JUDGE FOR YOURSELF

L A Naylor is part-time publications editor (and the administrator) of Children with AIDS Charity and is currently finishing a novel based on her experiences of working in rural Guatemala, entitled *The Craze in Creation*. She was granted an award in April 2002 by the Campaign for Learning Organisation to write *Judge for Yourself*.

Judge for Yourself

How many are innocent?

L A Naylor

ROOTS BOOKS

British Library Cataloguing in Publication Data
A catalogue record for this book is available from the British
Library

ISBN 0-9547437-0-9

Typeset by Amolibros, Milverton, Somerset
This book production has been managed by Amolibros
Printed and bound by Advance Book Printing, Oxford, England

CONTENTS

Simon Hattenstone at the Guardian

L.A Naylor has dedicated years to highlighting miscarriages of justice. In this book, she shows how the likes of Paddy Hill and Robert Brown were wrongly accused of murder and left to rot inside the system, and when they finally had their convictions overturned they were left without an apology, unsupported and often helpless in the "free" world. What is most alarming in all these cases is that either there was enough evidence to prove their innocence or insufficient evidence to convict. Naylor shows how once a miscarriage has happened the establishment closes in to prevent it being exposed. The book is at its most powerful when these lifers and former lifers tell their own devastating stories. Perhaps the strongest message to emerge is that there is no peace without justice. Anyone interested in Britain, social justice and human resilience should read this book.

Michael Mansfield QC

Each time a miscarriage of justice occurs, the government of the day announces reform and promises "no repetition". Over the years we have seen the introduction of the Police & Criminal Evidence Act [Pace] regulating the investigation of crime and the CCRC [Criminal Cases Review Commission] examining flawed convictions and the Auld Review of the Criminal Justice System as a whole. What this timely book demonstrates with telling clarity is that the risk of miscarriage has not diminished and that the human cost involved is incalculable. The examples used, and the stories told, are often those overlooked or marginalised by the policy makers and pundits, who categorise such material as anecdotal. At the end of the day, issues of serious non-disclosure or flawed forensic science need be measured in human terms. All of this requires urgent consideration in the light of the present Home Secretary's draconian proposals for restricting jury trial, lowering the standards of proof, admitting previous convictions, admitting hearsay, allowing intelligence information as evidence, in camera hearings with specially appointed Counsel etc. etc. This work should be essential and obligatory reading for all politicians and practitioners."

Dr Michael Naughton

This book is an extremely well written polemic that pulls no punches. It should be read by everyone and in particular anyone interested in criminology, sociology of law and criminal justice studies.

Acknowledgements

I have many people to thank. For a start this project would not have become reality without the kind support of the Campaign for Learning, an organisation working for an inclusive society in which learning is understood, valued and accessible to everyone as of right. Paddy Joe Hill inspired its creation with his unwavering support, ever-present strength, patience and clarity both as a friend and mentor. Trevor Jones at Cardiff University, a member of the British Society of Criminology commented on the manuscript and offered guidance despite a hectic schedule.

In particular my heartfelt thanks go to everyone who agreed to be interviewed, for giving me their time, trust and the confidence to write and to all at the Miscarriages of Justice Organisation (MOJO) for their professionalism and dedication to injustice. I also thank John O'Reilly from Miscarriages Of Justice United Kingdom (MOJUK) whose constant stream of articles, interaction with prisoners and networking with campaign groups on the web has been an education in itself. Without the support of law graduate Nikesh Shukla it is doubtful that Sue Lucas-MacMillan would have been able to feature her case in this book. His efforts to review her case, listening to her testimony during visits, reading through piles of paperwork and helping her write up her experiences were invaluable. He also contributed to her narrative. Thank you so much.

I'd like to express my love and thanks to other friends and family members: my mother for constantly telling me to hurry up and forever asking me if I'd finished 'it'; my father for offering advice and input and my brother Andrew for being my brother. I am also thankful to Deeder, Arun and Amena Zaman for reading some of the first drafts and responding with such enthusiasm. Rob Brown and Paul Blackburn, may the fire in your spirits burn forever and spread like wildfire through the veins of the prison system. This book is dedicated to all family and friends that mean so much to me: whoever you are and wherever you are.

Author's Note

It is 2004 and possible that you could get locked up in Britain for a crime you have not committed. This book places the issues and concerns of miscarriages of justice into context from the layperson's perspective. It explores not only how such miscarriages are created but also why they are perpetuated even when it is widely established that not all prisoners are guilty of the crimes for which they have been convicted. The book features material from a number of 'miscarriage' cases, those of human beings some of whom have spent more than twenty years in jail. Having challenged their convictions from day one, it is rare that prisoners are given a voice from within the wall of secrecy that surrounds their everyday existence, and, if innocent, their everyday nightmare.

A question is asked: when justice is contested, as it ultimately will be, given that no human-made system is infallible, how do we in society respond to these human beings, locked up in maximum security conditions for heinous crimes, pleading their eternal innocence?

Based on numerous interviews ranging from the prisoners themselves and their families, to government agency representatives, lawyers, campaigners, professors of criminology, QCs, MPs, musicians, the media and those who have since had their convictions overturned and been released, the book addresses this question and finds an uncomfortable answer.

These last three years have been a journey into completely new territory for me. My aim was to contact ten unrelated people who had served or were still serving long sentences for serious crimes such as murder –all of who denied guilt of the offence. Of these people, five had been released from prison after having served the sentence imposed upon them; five were still doing time. In this way I was able to encompass people at different stages of the prison and judicial systems.

To target these people I approached Hazel Keirle, the administrator of Miscarriages of Justice Organisation. I remember feeling astounded when she pointed to a huge filing cabinet and started pulling random files out. It was stuffed with an A-Z of over four hundred files. I picked out a few and as I started to read, I got the sense that I was slowly lowering myself by rope into a bottomless, dark pit, a claustrophobic, dank place where the sun rarely shone.

Weeks later I began the hit-and-miss task of writing to each prisoner and attempting to obtain access to their files, lawyers and any relevant newspaper articles. Visits were arranged. As stories slowly unravelled I went through case histories and asked questions. Burning questions remained unanswered, like: who are these people? If they are telling the truth then why are they still in prison? How did they come to be so stuck? What do they think? How do they behave? Who supports them?

Due to constraints in time and difficulty in obtaining access to all the prisoners, I focussed my limited resources on six individuals of differing age, background, gender and ethnic identity whom I hoped would be able to answer some of the above through informing me about their experiences. Chapters five and six are subsequently a collection of oral histories collated over time. When all six testimonies are compared, issues can be picked out that run through all the cases such as policing, forensics, trial and parole issues. This formed the basis for the first four chapters.

Drawing upon groundbreaking research conducted by prominent psychiatrists at the Institute of Criminology, the reader will be able to realise to some extent the nature and detail of long-term oppression and its adverse effects on prisoners after release. The book concludes with a call for responsible action, given that while there is no set of criteria that would make possible a common ground for ending injustice, it is up to society to acknowledge the 'miscarriages' now present in alarming numbers.

FOREWORD

Paddy Joe Hill

When I was asked to review this book and to write the foreword to it, I confess that I was a bit apprehensive. My main concern was due to the fact of my friendship with the author. I also knew that L A Naylor had been involved with other miscarriages of justice. My biggest fear was that her friendship with us may make the author slightly biased.

My first reading of the book surprised me. I was so relieved to find that there was no bias at all. My second reading took a lot longer – the reason for this was twofold. Firstly, as I was reading it I was getting angry – but my anger was not for me. It was for all the other INNOCENT people who are still locked up for nothing. The other reason was more heart-breaking. For a year I had been helping Robert Brown, who was released after twenty-five years. I watched him look after his dying mother and I relived once again the horrors of what Robert, I, and so many others have had to go through. I only wish that everyone could have seen it, because then maybe something would be done to stop miscarriages of justice from happening.

One of the things that the public find hard to understand is just how easy it is to be put in prison for a crime you did not commit. I am sure that before readers have finished this book they will have a better understanding.

This book invites readers to take part and to use their own intelligence – all the information you need is here. I recommend that every law student, solicitor, barrister, QC and judge should be made to read it. I have no doubt that if they did, we would not have as many miscarriages of justice as we have now.

I hope the author of this book gets the acclaim it deserves, as this is one of the best that has ever been written about miscarriages of justice.

Paddy Joe Hill, Birmingham Six

INTRODUCTION

On 14 March 2001, I was invited to the House of Commons by MOJO, set up by Paddy Joe Hill, one of the men more commonly known as the 'Birmingham Six'. It aims to help innocent people who find themselves wrongfully convicted and jailed for a crime for which they are not responsible. The date of MOJO's official launch coincided with the tenth anniversary of the release of Paddy and other members of the Birmingham Six. Convicted for the bombing of the Mulberry Bush and Tavern Bars in Birmingham in 1974, in which 21 people were killed and over 160 injured, all six were released in 1991 after the case against them was finally overturned.

My mind boiled with shock throughout the day as I listened to the speakers and became aware of what this meant – because what it meant was that Paddy had been locked up and punished for seventeen whole years, for something he had not done. It meant irreversible, chronic and disabling post-traumatic stress syndrome and the tearing apart of his family. A leading psychiatrist and head of the Institute of Criminology at Cambridge, Dr Adrian Grounds, compared the mental state of miscarriage survivors with that of people who had suffered war crimes. Most scary of all, I slowly began to realise that it could happen to anyone, including me.

What became painfully obvious to me, a lay person, unskilled in the workings of the law, was how incredibly little has been done to prevent more innocent lives from being destroyed since the release of the Birmingham Six. Protection of the law *still* stops dead at the prison gates, even when it has been established that many people incarcerated in there are not guilty of the crimes for which they have been convicted. That miscarriages of justice continue to occur in today's British criminal justice system is beyond doubt. No human-made system is infallible. But until we directly experience injustice ourselves, for the most part we remain blissfully unaware of the sheer scope of its shortcomings.

Other than the occasional impassioned story in the press that covers the release of a miscarriage case after a record-breaking stint of jail time and a long-ago sensational murder trial that we can barely remember, we have no personal comparison to make of the pain caused to the wrongfully convicted. We have no understanding of the legal pitfalls to be avoided for the future generation of inevitable miscarriages. Least of all do we feel responsible. Yet, if we did understand the 'miscarriage', I do have faith in humanity that we would stand together to do something radical about it.

The first crucial fact to learn is this: The 'miscarriage of justice' does not differentiate between colour, gender, creed or class and can happen to any single one of us. It can even happen to a white, middle-class solicitor, as shown by the recent case of Sally Clark. Clark was convicted of murdering two of her children and recently acquitted by the Court of Appeal (CA).

In today's society it is not unreasonable to assume that there is an appropriate strategy in place to take care of every type of system failure. Aeroplane crash scenes are studied in minute detail by aviation authorities so that future tragedies do not occur. If a patient dies during medical surgery, we can be sure an investigation will take place so that the cause may be determined. Incredibly, legal authorities working within the criminal justice system make no real effort to collect, organise and properly review their errors, namely the injustice of wrongful conviction. It was my mother who taught me that we human beings make mistakes in order to learn from them. Like anyone else I do not like to be wrong, but try to better myself by examining my own howlers as an unruly youth and onwards.

I'd never before seen a House of Commons room so congested with people. My only other experience of entering this formidable building had been to attend a conference on racism. Barely twenty people had turned up, and nearly all of them had been people of colour from various anti-racist groups. On the tenth anniversary of Paddy's release, the room heaved with bodies of all creeds, colours and professions.

Waiting for the official start of the conference, I could not help feeling delighted for the organisers. A good turn-out signalled a great deal of support, but as I learnt who it was that made up this room of people, initial elation was slowly replaced with shaky misgivings. By the time the last speaker had finished, I was well and truly gutted. Snapped out of astonishment by Paddy announcing the interval, I glanced at my watch and stumbled out of that room, racing past the impassive security guards, suddenly realising that my car had probably been clamped by the preying Westminster hit squad of parking attendants.

What made my stomach churn most was that such a huge, desperately needed task could actually have been left to the damaged *victim* of a gross injustice to carry out. That entailed setting up an organisation that was willing to care professionally for miscarriages upon release, and review wrongful convictions in order to attempt correction of errors. We are after all talking about truth, law and justice here, the three intrinsic factors central to making our society what it is today.

I had previously been introduced to Paddy by press officer John McManus, and while determined to offer whatever help I could, I remember also thinking to myself that surely organisations already existed out there that did the kind of thing that MOJO planned to do. Given that it was now ten years since Paddy's release, lawyers and judges should have long ago organised together to make sure that this kind of thing could at least be more swiftly dealt with than the seventeen years it took Paddy to get out. Surely by now, housing, counselling and compensation needs should have been taken care of while Parliament went about changing legislation to prevent further miscarriages from taking place. Given the psychologically damaged and completely institutionalised, tattered remains of lives that walked out of prison ten years ago, could it really be that *nothing* had been done?

My attendance at the House of Commons confirmed all this and much more. High-profile solicitors such as Gareth Pierce were present, as well as QCs Michael Mansfield, Helena Kennedy, and other barristers. MPs John McDonnell and Neil Gerard were there as well as law lecturers, psychiatrists, forensic pathologists and numerous journalists. It must be true then: Ten years had passed since the Birmingham Six were released yet no one in the government or Parliament, no judges, no committed band of lawyers or professors, not one of these authorities had bothered to carry out a detailed analysis that considered the needs and experiences of victims of miscarriages of justice, and changed the system accordingly. Or perhaps they had tried to do so and failed.

Paddy himself had long ago stopped expecting any collective form of professional help; when I met him he was *still* fighting his own case thirty years on, crazy as that may sound. The most naïve of us would assume that the Birmingham Six would have each retired by now on an £8 million or so compensation deal, but this couldn't be further from the truth.

As long as judges, lawyers and MPs appear to present themselves as arrogant dopes, willing to believe wholeheartedly in the integrity of our police forces, prisons and criminal justice system, it remains for the nation at large to acknowledge the disaster that is the 'miscarriage of justice', present now in huge numbers in our society.

This book invites you to examine the current process by which you may find yourself convicted of a crime for which you are not responsible. It will relate the stories of three victims of miscarriages of justice incarcerated at various prisons around the country, and three people who have since been released. It will talk about the nature and uncomfortable detail of oppression, as it is inevitably the oppressed that suffer injustice. It will conclude with a logical call to action. By the end of this book I hope to have opened minds to the disquieting knowledge that far from reducing crime, our criminal justice system actually generates it by placing over 3,000 wrongfully convicted people a year into prison while allowing the guilty to go free. This estimate was reported in a Home Office bulletin, while a recent report by the Prison Reform Trust (PRT) showed that in 2002 alone, almost 12,000 people were held on remand in prison until proven innocent.

For reasons of practicality this book attempts to provide a voice for prisoners who have been convicted of the most serious crimes such as murder. The only exception is the case of Mark Barnsley, due to the fact that he received a sentence equal in length to those convicted of murder, though he was convicted of grievous bodily harm.

All have been to the CA and their convictions have been upheld. As Hazel Keirle, MOJO's administrator states:

> Then you're a victim of a miscarriage of justice because in terms of challenging your conviction you've got nowhere to go. Technically, if you've been wrongfully convicted, as far as *I'm* concerned you're a miscarriage of justice in the strict sense of the word. But then how many people in prison have been to the Appeal Court and failed? If you included everyone who hadn't even appealed yet, you couldn't cope. I have no idea of how many people have been wrongfully convicted in the magistrate courts. But because the penalty is not so hard they take it at the time and are more able to get on with their lives afterwards. But they're just as much a victim of a miscarriage of justice as anybody else.

In theory there is somewhere for prisoners to turn after losing an appeal or being refused leave to appeal. The CCRC was set up following such miscarriage of justice cases as the Birmingham Six, Guildford Four, Tottenham Three, Judith Ward and Stefan Kiszko. These people's experiences, when finally exposed following public scrutiny, raised serious issues of concern to all, and greatly undermined public confidence in both the judicial and prison systems when the arrangements for criminal justice so completely failed, destroying lives in the process.

The Royal Commission's report was presented to Parliament in July 1993 and recommended the establishment of an independent body, which would consider suspected miscarriages of justice, arrange for their investigation and refer unsafe cases back to the CA.

The Criminal Appeal Act 1995 was subsequently passed, enabling the establishment of the CCRC as an executive non-departmental public body on 1 January 1997. The commission started handling casework from 31 March 1997, and at the time of writing is chaired by senior freemason Frederick Crawford. Its level of efficiency is examined in Chapter 3.

Thousands of people in Britain are sick and tired of seeing friends or family members go to prison for crimes they have not committed, only to spend indefinite years fighting the system to get them out again. However, it isn't enough just to be informed about such things these days. This is an interactive book and the reader is invited to take part. Whether banker, doctor, lawyer, MP, teacher, accountant, sales executive, or campaigner, our attitudes have shifted and the public conscience has no choice but to drag law and justice, amid a huge network of direct action if necessary, into modern-day expectations of accountability and fairness.

The ethics in this book are guided by one simple thing only: every human being has the right to live a decent life. Any establishment that systematically serves to deny that right without evidence of reasonable cause is a danger to society and should be reformed pronto. It does not take a genius to follow these ethics nor to analyse evidence.

I ought also to add that my putting together this book was not about undermining public confidence in the criminal justice system any further than it has undermined itself already. I am not hell-bent on destroying the system – I merely wish to fill some of that void between academics who know much about the system and those who know nothing until it is too late.

There is no point in feeling overcome with despair of ever finding solutions in the face of the power the judges and police wield over the 'common' citizen, especially when so many of us all feel the same way about things. Why not judge the system and call it into question instead?

1

THE CREATION OF A MISCARRIAGE OF JUSTICE

Innocent, law-abiding members of the public can be locked up for very many years at the drop of a hat. Committing an offence is not a necessary prerequisite. Miscarriages of justice occur for many reasons: because the police or prosecution has not disclosed evidence; evidence is fabricated; witness statements may be false or involve mistaken eyewitness identification; confessions are unreliable due to police pressure or psychological instability. A judge, chosen by the establishment rather than being democratically elected, may misdirect a jury or even sleep through court proceedings.

The psychological effects of being on remand (in custody pending a trial) for a capital offence when innocent, hinders the defendant's ability to conduct a strong defence, as fear and traumatic stress set in. Isolated from friends and family, housed with dangerous inmates and frequently denied access to legal advisers, there is no one to turn to for help. If in prison for the first time, the defendant will no doubt be in a state of shock and

..ientation. A recent review of remand prisoners, ιdertaken by HM Inspector of Prisons, stressed that some prisoners

...barely saw the light of day outside their cells

and that they were denied

...reasonable opportunities to sustain mental and physical health.[1]

So much for being innocent until proven guilty.

The Evolution of Policing

Policing has always involved, in one form or another, the exercise of power against someone and ultimately it is the police who decide if and when to use force, and how much to use. It is a weird but true fact that policing actually evolved with many decent policies in mind in the hope that some kind of public consensus could be achieved that favoured their existence.

Policies included a strategy for the use of minimum force, not to be seen as political in nature. The police were supposed to be accountable to the courts and able to *identify* more with the British public than with the state. The influence of social, economic and political climates meant that by the 1950s the police had changed from being a loathed and feared institution, into one that was widely accepted as being a legitimate authority.[2] This wasn't to last for long though.

Huge problems arise for any democratic society

supposedly trying to govern the police by the rule of law, by virtue of the fact that the police have the power (rightly or wrongly) to exercise legitimate force. Much of their work, such as street-level policing, is not immediately observable, and neither is it open to legal scrutiny or in fact any form of accountability. As a result there are very few safeguards in place to protect the citizen from wrongful arrest or police corruption, when it arises.[3]

The codes of practice that used to govern police behaviour were known as the Judges' Rules, and were introduced to Britain in 1912. They attempted to strike a semblance of balance between police powers and the rights of the suspected citizen. Under these rules, threatening behaviour and the coercion of individuals were forbidden. While under arrest, people were supposed to be cautioned before questioned and told that they could consult with a solicitor.[4]

The courts permitted continuous breaches of the rules to the extent that fabricated statements and false confessions have been a wide feature of admissible evidence in recent history. Trial judges sometimes acted as if they could not care less that suspects were supposed to be guaranteed access to legal advice. Senior judges preferred to believe that defence lawyers simply impeded the process of evidence gathering and did not consider it important to afford citizens any kind of protection from undue (or corrupt) contact with the police.[5]

In 1977 a Royal Commission on Criminal Procedure was finally established, as case after case was exposed as having been built on pretence. The Maxwell Confait case in particular caused outrage when the public learnt that three mentally impaired, vulnerable teenagers had been wrongfully convicted of his murder. The purpose of the Royal Commission was to clarify and review the law governing police powers, having regard for how innocent members of the public ought to be protected.[6]

In 1984 the legal regime was incorporated into the Police and Criminal Evidence Act (PACE) and it was hoped that this legislation would prevent more miscarriages of justice from occurring. Police investigators were provided with constraints on how long they could interrogate suspects for. Interviews had to be taped to avoid forced confessions and the beating or intimidation of suspects. Arrested suspects now have the absolute right to get legal advice, which is free, and the police have a duty to inform suspects of their rights.

The Home Secretary issued a set of codes of practice under PACE, in an attempt to ensure that procedures were followed while dealing with suspects. Breaching them however is not a criminal offence. It makes people like me wonder why the hell they bothered.

The Royal Commission recommended that arrest, being a coercive power, should not be an automatic matter of course and that far greater reliance should be placed on the summons procedure. The sad reality is that far more people are arrested post-PACE than were being arrested pre-PACE. McConville et al, researching this element in the 1980s, demonstrated that the summons procedure was used in a mere two per cent of all cases.[7]

Instead of reducing arrest, PACE seems to have brought about a dramatic increase in its use. The lives of thousands of innocent people, who are placed on remand and are lucky enough to be acquitted at trial, have been totally destroyed. People often lose their jobs, their homes and their partners as a result of imprisonment. Not surprisingly, they are often left feeling distraught as well as deeply distrustful of the police.

Research studies have shown that post-PACE, only a minority of suspects actually secure legal advice at the police station. When Sanders et al conducted their research in the mid-1980s, only fourteen per cent of people under arrest obtained legal advisers and they suspect that little has changed today.[8] Access to a solicitor is not automatic. It has to be requested and it isn't uncommon for police officers to try and dissuade a suspect from securing help, on the basis that they'll end up having to spend much longer in the station waiting for a solicitor to arrive. Other suspects – in the knowledge that they are innocent – may display a degree of misguided confidence. They believe the police will let them go as soon as they've established that there's been a mistake. The police however may fail to get this far in their 'investigation'.

Frequently, solicitors are a complete waste of time and don't actually serve any constructive purpose even when they do come down to the station. They will assume guilt without taking the time to chat to the suspect, effectively taking the unsuspecting suspect one step closer to wrongful imprisonment. Regrettably, only a few legal practices that specialise in criminal work place moral objectives to get at the truth of a matter over financial objectives. It took Stephen Downing twenty-eight years in prison before his conviction was overturned and it was finally agreed that Derbyshire Police had gained his confession unlawfully and under duress. Jane Hickman, secretary of the Criminal Appeal Lawyers' Association (CALA), has frequently highlighted ways in which defence lawyers are implicated in cases of miscarriages of justice.[9]

> They didn't know what the law was, which is pretty bad as these people are paid to be lawyers. They give inadequate advice at the police station, if any at all. You'll find a lack of engagement in the process of disclosure and breaches of the professional rules. You'll find that things weren't prepared for trial: witnesses weren't found and statements weren't taken.[10]

Paul Blackburn, at the time of writing, has served twenty-five years in prison, even though he alleges that the police gained confessions from three other suspects in their investigations. There is no forensic evidence to connect him to the crime.[11]

Academics have been greatly divided over the impact that PACE legislation has had in reducing the number of miscarriages of justice in Britain. Talk to any victim of injustice and one is left with a deep sense of foreboding that most aspects of the legislation haven't made the slightest dent on police behaviour. It is said that officers have merely crafted new means of manipulating written records and vulnerable suspects. Under this guise, the philosophies that lay behind the PACE regulations are dead and buried.

Dealing With Police Targeting and Corruption

I decided to start my quest for knowledge and understanding here, figuring that the police force acts as a kind of gateway to the rest of the criminal justice system. As certain subjects at school like law and order are not compulsory learning, it may surprise people to learn that police corruption in Britain is now considered to be commonplace. Drug testing and lie-detector tests for detectives have been considered by organisations such as the Association of Chief Police Officers (ACPO) and the Metropolitan Police as options in the struggle against corruption.[12]

On average, no more than 30 to 50 police officers out of a population of approximately 150,000 are convicted of a criminal offence each year. Usually this occurs when an accused officer has been caught red-handed and can't cover up his actions, yet even so it is rare that officers are ever made to take responsibility for their misconduct or corruption involving wrongful convictions. When the Birmingham Six attempted to bring a civil action against members of the police, whom they alleged had tortured false confessions out of them, the thankfully late Lord Denning committed gross abuse of power by deciding on behalf of 'every sensible person in the land' that their civil action be dismissed. He effectively assured corrupt police officers that they could continue to torture, kill and frame innocent people and get away with it. This they have done. Between 1969 and 1999 more than 1,000 people were killed while in custody yet not one officer of the law has been successfully prosecuted for a single death.[13]

In Britain the very idea of taking appropriate punitive action against the police for serious misconduct remains a figment of outlandish imagination. Not one accused officer arising from the miscarriage of justice cases since 1989 has been convicted of a criminal offence, yet there have been well over 150 high-profile cases released at the CA.

Christopher Stone, Director of the Vera Institute of Justice in New York, states that few prosecuting agencies in the world have either the resources or the commitment to devote specialised units to such cases on a routine basis.[14] The CPS is no exception and writer David Rose (1996) describes the failure of the Director of Prosecutions to act as being almost impossible to bear. Yet if the CPS believes that it is not in the interests of the state to prosecute and hold police officers accountable for their actions, it follows that the criminal justice system cannot function effectively or efficiently. The working class, people with learning difficulties and ethnic minorities continue to be sent to prison in disproportionate numbers and Britain has the highest rate of imprisonment in Western Europe. We have a wholly inadequate system made up of politicians, senior police officers and judges who moralise about how we should take responsibility for our actions and mistakes, yet they themselves never take moral responsibility for their own actions.

Drew Days, US Assistant Attorney General for Civil Rights between 1977 and 1980, believes that in the USA a caste system operates, and I am inclined to believe that the same applies in Britain to a certain extent. He says,

The Police, as an institution, pick their victims very carefully. They pick racial minorities, the poor, the homeless, homosexuals. They pick those who do not make very persuasive witnesses. So what you have is a nice, neat, well-spoken cop who says, 'I was doing my duty,' and a victim who is often inarticulate, often with a criminal record, and often without anybody to provide character support. This makes police misconduct cases even harder to win.[15]

Christopher Alder was aged thirty-seven when he died, handcuffed and face down in Hull Police Station in April 1998, surrounded by police officers after choking on his own vomit and blood. A commended paratrooper in Northern Ireland, he died helpless on the floor of the station with his trousers and pants pulled down to his ankles.[16]

Security camera videotapes allegedly captured his dying breaths amid the jokes and laughter of five officers. Alder was the father of two, black, and according to a coroner's jury unlawfully killed while held in police custody.

At Hull Royal Infirmary, police officers had arrested Alder and dragged him to a police van to take him to the police station. Paramedics had taken Alder to hospital earlier, after he was injured during an unrelated street quarrel, in which he was struck on the back of his head. It was with dismay and shock that the same paramedics returned to remove Alder's body from the station.

Investigators of the case took the custody-room videotapes away for examination and the five officers were suspended on full pay. The Alder family were to learn more disturbing details of his death. Christopher's clothes were destroyed before any forensic tests could be carried out on them, and the clothing worn by the officers was not forensically checked.

Worst of all perhaps was the manner in which the CPS attempted to prosecute the police officers involved. For four years, a vital section of the videotape was ignored, a section that allegedly contained monkey chants and was not studied until March 2002, just two weeks before the trial. Mr Enzor, head of the CPS Casework Directorate in York, admitted that the transcriber of the video footage, an expert in phonetics and applied linguistics had

> ...noted noises, which she considered sounded like a person or persons making chimpanzee or monkey like noises followed by laughter.

The CPS did not attempt to admit this evidence to the court because, it was said, they could not determine who (out of the five officers) was making the noises. Similarly, no jury was ever informed that Christopher's clothes had been destroyed. On 21 June 2002 Justice Roderick Evans dismissed charges of manslaughter and misconduct in a public office and the officers returned to duty. Lawyers acting for the Alder family will now take their case to the European Court of Human Rights, though it could be five years before the case is heard.

The judiciary have allowed police misconduct to flourish at our peril. According to a leaked document written by the National Criminal Intelligence Service (NCIS) in 1998, it is now commonplace for police officers to steal property and drugs during searches, plant drugs or stolen goods on individuals and destroy evidence.[17]

Michael Mansfield, QC, with his legendary success rate in high-profile civil liberties cases, and who represented the Birmingham Six, Judith Ward, the Tottenham Three and the family of Stephen Lawrence, among many other cases, has his own views on police corruption. He says,

> It's a failing that I've highlighted before but absolutely nothing has been done about it. It's really where the system begins because the bottom line is – what is the evidence that a court or a jury is looking at? That evidence is primarily gleaned and assembled by the police. Now what nearly all the miscarriage cases of the early 1990s demonstrated was a very primeval instinct that has permeated prosecutions from the beginning of time. Investigators, like it or not, have got a set of preconditions that they impose on a set of circumstances. In the case of the police it's what I've always, in the past, called targeting. They want to make things fit.

I asked Paddy for his views on police misconduct and was startled by his degree of objectivity. He said, almost hypnotising me with his steely, unblinking, ice blue glare:

> As far as the cops are concerned, I tell people that there are two police forces operating in the country. The vast majority of ordinary cops, most commonly known as uniformed PCs, I have a hard time defending because I don't envy them

in today's society. They always get stick and there are arseholes running around with knives, machine guns and meat cleavers and there are all sorts of junkies and screwballs runnin' around etc. Their job is very hard and there's no doubt about it, they have suffered a hell of a lot of injustice as far as miscarriages of justice are concerned.

This, from someone who has suffered torture at the hands of the police, left me somewhat astounded. 'Why?' I asked. He retorted,

Because they're not the people who put us in prison. What you must remember is the other side. It's the 25–30,000 so-called detective forces that need to be held accountable.

Did he mean the plain-clothed ones?

Exactly. They are the people that investigate serious crime not PC Plod. PC Plod comes in and has to knock on the door for them but they only gather the information. They pass it on, you understand? If the place belongs to someone, they take down the name. They only do the donkeywork, end of story. It's the others higher up who should be accountable. They're the ones who hide, distort or make up the evidence. I don't know what it is with half of them so-called detectives and it sickens and saddens me that they get away with it.

He shook his head in angry disgust and looked away.

Modern-day corrupt activities, placed into the nation's conscience by publicised cases, have involved the suppression of evidence, beating of suspects, tampering with and fabrication of evidence (otherwise known as 'flaking' or 'padding') and perjury. Other forms of corruption have been characterised by authors like Roebuck and Barker (1974), who identify eight types, ranging from kickbacks and shakedowns to internal payoffs. Whatever the definition, it is generally accepted that corruption necessarily involves an abuse of position and breach of trust. For the purposes of this book, police corruption is defined as the exploitation or misuse of authority, typically characterised by bribery, violence and brutality, the fabrication, destruction and planting of evidence.

Punch (1985) broadens the definition to include not only illegitimate but approved goals, otherwise known as 'noble cause corruption'. I fail to see how any form of corruption could be deemed noble, for even if the *goal* is noble, the means by which it is attained, if corrupt, can never guarantee achievement of that goal – unless one is prepared to move the goalposts.

Newburn was commissioned by the Policing and Crime Reduction Unit of the Home Office in 1999 to provide a common level of understanding of police corruption and its causes.[18] In the resulting body of work that he produced, however, he is not even sure whether it is helpful to include 'a procedural breach resulting in conviction' as a category of corruption. Admittedly, while it may be ambitious to attempt an all-inclusive definition (and Newburn also suggests that defining the essential characteristics of corruption is largely impossible), it is surely worth attempting to define and include those types that result in the wrongful conviction of citizens. How else can we quantify the problem and redress it? Imagine being wrongfully convicted for just a week, sent to a maximum-security prison and locked in a six-by-six-foot cell especially designed to oppress your every move during every hour of every day. Then magnify that by twenty-five years.

During the inner-city riots of the 1980s in London and Birmingham, groups of predominantly Asian and black but also white youths, fought pitched battles with police, tossing petrol bombs and bricks with all the pent-up frustration of a disenfranchised community. It was obvious that the police had problems relating to certain sections of the community, and the then government perceived this as a growing loss of public confidence in the police.

By 1993, the political mood on criminal justice had shifted enough to ignite public interest in the policy of policing, brought about by the numerous miscarriage-of-justice cases highlighting issues of gross police misconduct. Pressure on the police grew until public interest in policing policy reached a climax with the publication of the Royal Commission on Criminal Justice (also known as the Runciman Commission report). One of its aims was to consider whether changes in the conduct of police investigations were necessary.

Typically, the report did very little to affect policing policy and acted as a cushion merely to dissipate pressure on the police force to amend their corrupt ways. Reform can occur in organisations only if policies change and the police force is no exception. The riots in Burnley,

Bradford and Oldham in the summer of 2001 felt like déjà vu for those who had lived through the 'eighties. No one I know has great faith in the police as a service any more and I personally hold martial arts and my brave and faithful Rottweiler in far higher regard. But I want to know why there isn't any ongoing visible debate concerning efforts to tackle police corruption, by any of our policy makers.

We have witnessed a continual spate of miscarriage cases emerge from prison while thousands of other people are freshly condemned every year, at the end of farcical trials. Stephen Downing was wrongfully convicted of murder and jailed for twenty-eight years before finally being released on bail on 7 February 2001, pending an appeal. Frank Johnson was wrongfully convicted of murder and jailed for twenty-six years before being released suddenly on 26 June 2002, halfway through an appeal hearing. Satpal Ram was wrongfully convicted of murder and jailed for sixteen years before being released on 19 June 2002, following a court ruling that he had been unlawfully imprisoned. Mark Barnsley was wrongfully convicted of wounding with intent to cause grievous bodily harm and jailed for eight years before being released on 24 June 2002. Although the latter two men have challenged their convictions from day one, the CCRC has so far failed to refer their cases back to the CA.

Of those lifers who do eventually get their convictions overturned, there is no justice whatsoever in the form of redress, and yet what can be more of a crime than being forced to spend endless years locked up for something you never did? The only case that has ever been reopened and solved involved that of the Cardiff Three, but still not one police officer has been brought to book for any wrongdoing. The process of redress currently involves the police reinvestigating cases themselves and to borrow a phrase from Rob Brown, 'That's like the Third Reich investigating the SS for war crimes.'

Formal responsibility for the police is split in a tripartite structure between chief constables, the Home Secretary and local police authorities. The Home Office is the most influential body and up until 1999 the Home Secretary formed the police authority for the country's largest force, the Metropolitan Police, and was responsible for its funding. Many people argue that the Home Office is able to exert significant pressure on senior police officers by controlling their career opportunities. Others, such as campaigners, are of the view that the division of responsibility, split as it is, serves to blur the issues deliberately, hiding decision-making from view and disguising power structure and intent.

I was to come across an admirable study that had been commissioned by the Policy Studies Institute.[19] It aimed to analyse how the various contributors involved in police policy-making interacted to produce positive change in the operations of policing. Contributors included the Home Office, Home Secretary, police service, police authorities, pressure and community groups, lawyers and the media.

I am often told we live in a democratic society and the researcher, criminologist Trevor Jones, argued that when it came to defining democracy in a society, the ways in which public services interfered with and impinged upon the lives of citizens were more relevant than either Parliament or central government were. The police form a central public service in a modern state, supposedly there to protect our essential freedoms. To do so, they hold a monopoly over the legitimate use of force. David Bayley took this further by stating,

> Because the police are the most visibly coercive instrument of government, their actions powerfully influence whether government is perceived to be legitimate.

Jones et al distil a set of seven criteria for judging in what ways a system can be considered 'democratic'. They arrive at factors like: equity (services should be delivered fairly between groups and individuals); responsiveness (the police should be responsive to all groups, in terms of prioritising, allocating resources and choice of policing methods); information (should be regularly published and distributed); redress (dealing with incompetent or corrupt police officers); and participation (citizens should participate in discussing policing policies).

'Policy' is broadly and aptly defined as that which demonstrates a pattern of behaviour in policing. It may therefore include the practice of habitually disbelieving allegations made by women of rape, or that we have the right to defend ourselves from physical attack. It may be that prostitutes and people with learning difficulties may be routinely treated as scum during investigation, because they aren't regarded as credible witnesses. In this way Jones is cleverly able to ignore rhetorical 'stated' policies, because of what they are – meaningless. Similarly, that every citizen is equal under the law is a surreal principle that bears no influence on the real-life dishing-out of criminal justice.

Policies therefore exist that may not have been formally set out and agreed by anyone inside or out of the police forces. Jones studied how some of these policies are shaped and affected by the institutional framework that surrounds the police and links them to the other institutions of a democracy.

During this two-year study, modernised policing responses to rape were studied. Four police forces in England were reviewed, at national level. Where the ACPO withheld approval, letters were written to individual chief constables. Four agreed to cooperate out of a total of ten constables being approached. Informal interviews were held with senior officers, other officers, and civilian staff. Records of police-authority meetings were analysed and organisations that came into contact with the police (such as police consultative committees and voluntary groups) were reviewed. Finally, Jones et al carried out research within central government and Parliament, interviewing several Home Office officials and MPs.

The Home Office were found to have a strong influence on the development of policy and circulars were found to be a major instrument of policy change. Although the researchers were not allowed privileged access to Home Office files, they did not find it difficult to trace the origins of circulars nor the process of consultation prior to a circular being sent out. Regrettably, they were to find out that none of the circulars arose from the concerns or interests of ministers. Officials merely awaited favourable political conditions before distributing proposals. In circulars on rape, officials were found to be responding to stimuli from pressure groups.

Circulars only emerged from the Home Office in final

form after considerable consultation with other bodies. Although the ACPO would not cooperate with the research, Jones is certain that they were consulted in every case and were 'virtually the joint authors of circulars on rape'. The role of pressure groups had been to initiate activity in these areas but they were not invited to take part in the detailed drafting of circulars.

HM Inspectorate of Constabulary, police authorities, staff associations and trade unions were found to have played no part in initiating policy change, though trade unions did influence policy by collective bargaining over issues of pay.

Police-community consultative committees, set up following recommendations made by Lord Scarman as a result of the 'eighties' riots, were also found to have negligible influence. Such committees are meant to represent the views of the community but rarely do so. Radicals believe that committees were set up in order to maintain an element of legitimacy on police actions, while actually keeping their decision-making autonomy intact.

The research led Jones et al to conclude firmly that Parliament too had only a very limited effect on policy change. Interviewing the late Jo Richardson, MP, who campaigned for many years on women's issues, she had made no strong claims about her influence, or that of any other MPs, on policy developments in the 1980s.

The law and its wider constitutional framework were found to influence the pattern of policing and the behaviour of individual officers in only an indirect way too. It is common knowledge that existing legal regulations are frequently ignored and a large body of research points to the fact that many rules exist merely to give an acceptable appearance to the manner in which police work is carried out. The introduction of PACE has not meant that investigative procedures are hugely different from what they were pre-PACE. In the miscarriage-of-justice case involving the Cardiff Three, officers believed they were working within PACE measures, but the courts disagreed. Confessions were excluded and acquittals followed when the judge commented that he was 'horrified' by the oppressive interrogations that had taken place.[20]

In the tragic case of Christopher Alder, one of the police officers held the rank of sergeant. Campaigners who have looked into the Objective Structured Performance Related Examination (OSPRE) sergeant's examination will know that in order to pass the exam, he would have been trained to know the requirements, under Section 9 of PACE, for the treatment and welfare of detainees. It most certainly does not involve allegedly mocking detainees while they choke to death with their trousers pulled down to the ankles.

Sanders (1999) argued that the codes of practice of PACE have altered the way that police officers account for their exercise of discretion, without changing the way they actually exercise it. Paddy Hill adds that police officers now have a greater incentive to 'practise' interviews with suspects by interrogating them in the cells first, or in the back of cars before reaching the station. Given that police officers routinely escape punishment for wrongdoing in our courts, it is little wonder that many have come to view the law as a means of distancing the police from control by anyone. This is hardly democratic.

Crucially, what the study demonstrated was that the two main influences in stimulating policy change in police responses to rape were that of women's pressure groups and the media. Women's organisations were basing their views and demands for change on a body of research and analysis that had formed over two decades. National publicity supported their views. There is also widespread agreement that a particular programme transmitted in 1982 by Roger Graef had helped to instigate change. It showed a woman being interviewed by two disbelieving CID officers and the impact of the programme was so great that it caused a massive public reaction. The filming and broadcasting of a case succeeded in revealing what was wrong with the standard police investigation of rape. That the Home Office felt obliged to issue a circular that year on rape investigation is telling.

What of police corruption then? Who is going to initiate changes in policing policies in an effort to crack down on the number of innocent citizens that are targeted and charged for crimes they haven't committed? The lessons to be drawn from research by Jones et al are that police officers, when under pressure, can come to view situations differently, yet institutions like Parliament and police authorities may have very little influence. Nor does policy change typically involve participation of the wider public or representative bodies, except in a media sense. Perhaps to some extent this is why progressive change is so slow. The formal democratic institutions that are supposed to frame policing do not appear to have played an important role in initiating modernised police responses to rape.

Democracy is not only about our institutions and the way they interact with each other to instigate change, but more importantly is about the openness of society, and our ability as a whole to respond to new demands and pressures. It now made perfect sense to me that someone like Paddy Hill should be the one to set up a miscarriages-of-justice organisation, though no less remarkable. I quote once again from leaked documents by the NCIS. The documents form the minutes of a meeting on police corruption, attended by Britain's top policy makers. 'Corrupt police officers exist throughout the UK police service,' reported Roger Gaspar, the then Director of Intelligence. He admitted that corruption had become 'pervasive' and may have reached 'level 2': the situation occurring in some Third World countries.

It gets worse. Such corruption is deliberately concealed from the public because 'adverse publicity' could erase some of the ideology we're fed about the police. The minutes request that ACPO formulate a strategy to deal with any negative publicity. Indeed, a month after the meeting was held, the then president of ACPO, David Blakey, announced to the press,

> The true level of corruption in the modern police service is extremely low.

It seems the rule of silence extends to some of our policy makers, as well as our boys in blue. This is nothing short of a disaster because if corrupt police behaviour remains hidden, unacceptable behaviour can and will breed. Sherman and Reiner have long argued that police officers are socialised into not cooperating with investigations of their colleagues. Not only do honest police officers become conditioned to accept corruption as an inevitable part of the job, corrupt officers have a great means of pressuring fellow officers to join in. Secrecy is protective armour, not unlike that which the freemasons enjoy, and serves to shield the force as a whole from public knowledge of misconduct. Extend this to any of our policy makers and there is no way that one can seriously refer to Britain's current political environment as being democratic.

Internal accountability is one thing but those that engage in corruption will never take the lead in the fight against it. Corrupt police agencies are incapable of taking measures to prevent or even reduce corruption, because by definition it isn't in their interests. It would only be in excessive circumstances, which threaten to draw public attention to police corruption in general, that measures would be taken.

Sir John Stevens, himself Commissioner of the Metropolitan Police, is exasperated by the lack of judicial support shown by senior judges and the Director of Prosecutions in tackling the problems of police corruption. He recently admitted,

> Prosecution has proved difficult. Defendants, who as police officers know the system very well, have sought every opportunity to challenge all aspects of their case. There is on occasion *nothing* these people will not do in discrediting individuals.

His deputy, Ian Blair agreed, adding,

> Some defendants will play every trick in the book to avoid going to trial.[21]

In the past four years the Metropolitan Police has spent more than £20 million on anti-corruption work and has a squad of detectives investigating police corruption. In that time fifty-five officers have been charged, yet just twenty-six officers have been convicted. Sir John Stevens insists,

> There's no way on God's earth that you can get rid of corruption with the temptations that there are. The way of prevention is the certainty of discovery and a considerable prison sentence.

I feel it is ironic that Toby Harris, Chair of the Metropolitan Police Authority, can speak of 'democratic policing', and 'police accountability' as if the meanings were crystal clear and virtuous beyond question. Not that I would expect him to travel to a conference in Durban, South Africa as he did in December 2001 and talk about how corrupt our system of policing was. But his remarks do leave a chill in the air, when you consider that our policy makers have secretly compared levels of police corruption in Britain to that which occurs in some developing countries. He said:

> A police service must be democratically accountable. It cannot operate successfully without the implicit consent of the people it polices, or without the explicit consent of a democratically elected government. If both consents are not present, then the police become nothing less than a controlling force, an oppressive instrument of powerful self-interested

groups. In parts of the world this will be the military, in others local war lords, and in some the senior officers in the police force itself. If policing is thus distorted or dictated to by unrepresentative groups, the trust of the public is gone. The only possible result is a downward spiral that manifests itself in corruption, organised crime and abuses of human rights.[22]

Our policy makers ought to be willing to admit to the public how extensive the problems of police corruption are. As long as they don't, solutions will remain out of reach and there will be a continual decrease in the level of legitimacy accorded the police, and the degree of respect reserved for the judiciary and state officials themselves. For those like Paddy Hill, whose lives have been wrecked by the gross misconduct of the police and judiciary, there is but one view of the police service:

You could take some of our police detectives up in an aeroplane and strip them bollock naked and drop them off in the fuckin' North Pole and they're that useless they couldn't catch a fuckin' cold never mind a fuckin' criminal. They are totally and utterly useless. They're a disgrace to the force. And unfortunately these are the people that bring so much discredit to the force. And bring so much distress and suspicion towards the ordinary bobby on the beat whose job is made not doubly hard but triply hard by the stigma that's attached to them. Because of the Birmingham Six, Guildford Four, Cardiff Three,

Tottenham Three and all the others. I don't have any scruples about jumping on bad cops because I think it's not only in my interest, it's in the interests of society, Parliament, and the police in particular. And the one thing the police must accept is that they can only police with our consent. There's so much distrust with what's gone on in the past and still going on today, that people trust them less and less. And it's getting worse.

Note: all cited websites are current at the time of publication.
1 The full report, 'Unjust Deserts: A Thematic Review by HM Inspector of Prisons of the Treatment and Conditions for Unsentenced Prisoners in England and Wales' (2000) can be found at: www.homeoffice.gov.uk/docs/unjust.pdf.
2 McConville, M., Wilson, G., eds, *The Handbook of the Criminal Justice Process* (Oxford University Press, 2002).
3 Ibid.
4 Rose, D., *In the Name of the Law* (Vintage, 1996).
5 Ibid.
6 Walker, C., Starmer, K., eds, *Miscarriages of Justice, A Review of Justice in Error* (Blackstone Press Ltd, 1999).
7 McConville, M. et al, *The Case for the Prosecution* (Routledge, 1991).
8 Sanders, A., Bridges, L., Mulvaney, A. and Crozier, G., *Advice and Assistance at Police Stations & the 24 Hour Solicitor Scheme* (Lord Chancellor's Department, 1989).
9 Solicitor Jane Hickman was a guest speaker at MOJO's Second Annual Meeting, 12 March 2003.
10 Ibid.
11 Interview with the author. See also Jessel, D., *Trial and Error* (Headline, 1994).

12 *The Daily Telegraph*, 27 September 1998..

13 Directed by Fero, K., and Mehmood, T., *Injustice* (Migrant Media, 2001) is a ninety-eight minute documentary. For further details visit www.injusticefilm.co.uk.

14 Agathocleous, A., Ward, H. (with contributors), *Prosecuting Police Misconduct, Reflections on the Role of the US Civil Rights Division* (Vera Institute of Justice, USA, 1998).

15 Ibid.

16 *BBC News*, 15 April 2002. See also press releases by Inquest, an organisation investigating deaths in custody, found at www.inquest.org.uk and the website for the United Friends and Family Campaign, www.uffc.org.

17 *The Daily Telegraph*, op cit.

18 Newburn, T., 'Understanding and preventing police corruption: lessons from the literature' (Police Research Series Paper 110 (RDS Directorate, Home Office, 1999).

19 Jones, T., Newburn, T., Smith, D. J., *Democracy and Policing* (Policy Studies Institute, 1994).

20 Sekar, S., *Fitted In, The Cardiff 3 and the Lynette White Inquiry* (The Fitted In Project, 1997).

21 *The Independent*, 29 August 2002.

22 Speech by Toby Harris, Chair, Metropolitan Police Authority, *Police Accountability in a Democratic Society,* 5 December 2001.

2

THE CROWN PROSECUTION SERVICE (CPS)

Disclosure of Evidence

When the police decide to offer a case for prosecution, the defendant is charged and the case papers are handed over to the CPS, which reviews the evidence and makes a decision on whether or not to prosecute.

The CPS was set up in 1986 when it took over responsibility of prosecution from the police in England and Wales. Sometimes referred to in literature as an 'independent' body, we must remember that the CPS remains totally dependent on police investigations for the materials and information required to do the job. They prepare cases for court and form a central part of the criminal justice system, working in conjunction with the police, courts, and other agencies. They are supposed to prosecute cases fairly and effectively, when there is sufficient evidence to provide a realistic prospect of conviction, and when it is in the public interest to do so. The head of the CPS is the Director of Public Prosecutions, at the time of writing David Calvert-Smith, QC. The Attorney General, who is accountable to Parliament for the service, supervises him.

It has long been acknowledged by people working with miscarriage-of-justice cases that one of the underlying causes in most cases is the issue of non-disclosure of evidence to the defence. Naturally, any police investigation will build up a pile of material consisting of witness statements and scientific reports. Police disclosure officers decide what information should be disclosed to the crown prosecutors, even though they aren't legally trained to do so and despite the knowledge that many officers will stoop to any form of misconduct to obtain a conviction. The evidence that the police have assembled will often not be challenged until the trial, and as history shows us, defendants have a better chance of flying to the moon than making successful accusations of dishonesty against the police.

Undisclosed evidence is referred to as 'unused material' and can contain vital information that would undermine the case for the prosecution and greatly assist the accused. Paddy Hill reiterates the extent of the problem.

> One of the biggest problems we have is in respect of the role of the leading police officer in the case. His role now is not only to head the investigation but he has the right to decide what is evidence and what is not. He has the right to decide what, if any of it, can be disclosed to the public defence. It is not in the interests of the police to disclose evidence that would clear their suspects. Not

when they want to convict and have targeted whom they believe to be guilty of a crime.

So we live by a system whereby the wrongly accused may go to trial without the crucial evidence that would secure their acquittals. To add to this of course is the daunting fact that when a prosecution is brought by the state, the resources available to the prosecuting authorities outweigh by far those of all but the most affluent defendants, in terms of investigative, forensic and legal back-up.

In 1992, Judith Ward's conviction for the M62 coach bombings was quashed by the CA, amid a litany of examples of inappropriate non-disclosure by the prosecution, police and forensic experts. During the substantial media coverage that the case received, judges firmly endorsed the principle that defendants should have the same access to documents and records that the prosecution had. In practice, this attitude would bring about additional work, as both prosecutors and police had administrative duties to disclose unused statements. Strategic advantages long enjoyed by police and prosecutors were on the verge of being reduced.

The expected increase in work, without the support of adequate funds with which to carry it out, meant that it wasn't long before police and prosecutors began to complain. Many insisted that they were being forced to spend large amounts of money on supplying the defence with irrelevant material. Given that not one police officer would be held responsible for any of the high-profile miscarriage cases involving police misconduct, successful appeals were nastily branded 'technical' triumphs, the implication being that defendants were unmeritorious. If the police were found not guilty of misconduct, then the defendants must have been guilty all along.

The government and colluding judges instantly played on such a narrow-minded view, as the political environment struggled to bring back public confidence in the system, ignoring factual concerns. Where the Attorney General had previously approved the process of reciprocal disclosure in guidelines, there was a new drive towards 'the efficient use of resources', i.e. cost effectiveness and efficiency.

The Criminal Procedure and Investigations Act (CPIA), formed in 1996, created an obligation on the defendant to issue a defence statement. The aim of this legislation was to

> ...effectively bring about acquittal of the innocent and conviction of the guilty, while ensuring efficiency in focussing on key issues at trial and fairness towards all those affected.

Once the defence statement was passed over, the prosecution would then hand over

> ...any prosecution material which had not previously been disclosed to the defence and which in the prosecutor's opinion might undermine the case against the accused.

The scales of justice were once again tipped in favour of the state as the act allows the police to withhold material from the defence. Additional funds that were allocated to the CPS to meet the extra costs of operating the act went directly into salary increases for existing staff rather than the creation of new positions as envisaged in the explanatory and financial memorandum published with the bill. By the year 2000, various studies commissioned by members of the legal community had revealed widespread poor practice of disclosure.[1]

In recent research, 'A fair balance? Evaluation of the operation of disclosure law', by Joyce Plotnikoff and Richard Woolfson, eighty-two per cent of judges and a startling thirty per cent of senior police officers felt it unrealistic to expect police disclosure officers to identify undermining material. During the inspection of police schedules of material, seventy-three per cent of schedules were classified as 'poor' in that they were undated, or incomplete. There were no quality assurance structures in place other than checks to ensure that schedules were present on the file. There was a widespread failure to include relevant material in the schedules. Out of 121 crown court cases, only forty-five per cent had unused material disclosed to the defence.[2]

Rather than listen to the legal community – those that had every justification for warning about the potential for miscarriages of justices that this legislation created – the Attorney General instead issued yet more guidelines on disclosure and the Home Office commissioned yet more research. Roger Ede, secretary of the Law Society's Criminal Law Committee, has attempted to explain the severity of the situation.

By the time their research is complete, over a quarter of a million people will have been prosecuted and convicted under these provisions, after pleading not guilty in the magistrates and crown courts, yet we know the process by which they will have been tried is not working fairly.

Miscarriages of justice are *still* happening every day. More research commissioned by the Home Office has revealed that eighty-eight per cent of barristers, eighty-seven per cent of defence solicitors and sixty-one per cent of judges are dissatisfied with the way CPIA is operating. Relevant information continues to exist in many locations without ever becoming part of a prosecution file. Anthony Heaton-Armstrong and David Corker, themselves lawyers, say their research has revealed

> ...an alarming picture of incompetence, poor training, pig-headedness, blatant obstruction and generally a widespread inability amongst police and prosecution authorities to comprehend and put into practice the rules on disclosure.

Complaints that evidence undermining prosecution cases had been deliberately withheld from the defence were 'alarmingly frequent'.

It is impossible to calculate how many wrongful convictions have occurred as a result of this act. No one knows how much relevant material is being withheld in CPS offices and police warehouses. Suffice to say that legal experts working with MOJO currently hold 500 live prisoner cases alleging miscarriages of justice. In spite of a well oiled methodology whereby a detailed questionnaire is given to the prisoner and probing questions follow, eventually serving to weed out the real cases from those trying to play the system, this figure is rising every day. With limited resources, MOJO restrict their assistance to crown court cases only, but remain overwhelmed by requests for help and the alarming substandard details of cases they receive. And they have only been up and running for a little over three years.

Quality of Forensic Science Evidence

The Forensic Science Service (FSS) website, at the date of writing, represents a nationwide network of scientists regarded as expert witnesses, and every single one of its press releases promotes greater reliance upon forensic science to provide the necessary evidence against criminality.[3]

The advent of DNA profiling with its many phases of technique development has resulted in such examinations becoming widely available and relevant to investigations. On the surface, the identification of DNA definitely appeals on a variety of levels. Human errors can be avoided and thus so can miscarriages of justice. It conjures up the image of laboratory technicians in white coats erring on the side of caution with precision and detachment – a far cry from trying to determine the validity of evidence produced by traumatised memory during an identity parade.

At the earliest stages of a police investigation the forensic scientist is a specialist adviser who will often attend a crime scene, looking for clues and materials of evidential value that will serve to piece together exactly what happened. They offer advice as to where to proceed next in the investigation, taking on an active role.

When items arrive at the laboratory the scientist decides what to examine and test, depending on the amount and quality of information he or she has received. A written report will provide details of what the scientist considers to be of most use to the investigation. Like the police however, their objectivity is often weighed against their input and knowledge of the case.

Sometimes the forensic scientist will find it hard to decide what to study at the scene of a crime and what opinions to draw from the test results. It is not uncommon for different forensic scientists presented with the same sets of data to arrive at different conclusions. So there is always room for doubt. Unfortunately for both the lay observer and the legal expert, these can seem non-existent, cloaked from view by an impression of scientific accuracy and precision.

The increased applications of DNA analyses on saliva, skin tissues, blood, hair and semen are widely used as a reliable means of linking people to crimes. Until recently, fingerprint evidence in particular was regarded as foolproof. Juries commonly accept fingerprint evidence without question while defence lawyers rarely challenge its validity. Indeed, no two people have the same fingerprints.

The defence also uses forensic services, in order to clarify information received from scientists acting on behalf of the police or the prosecution and to provide a check on the results. Michael Mansfield has asserted that lawyers often aren't sure which particular branch of forensic science is relevant to a case. He supported Kevin Callan, a lorry driver who was charged with murdering his stepdaughter. Callan was convicted on evidence provided by pathologists when it was neurosurgeons who had the necessary expertise to prove his innocence.[4]

The fact that the wrong experts may be called to give evidence in cases may largely be due to the curious fact that Britain lacks educational forensic science facilities at university level for the budding lawyer. The result means that lawyers are not adequately equipped with the knowledge to cross-examine forensic evidence nor understand its meaning and significance. This is another recipe for miscarriages of justice.

Four factors are important to consider where forensic evidence is concerned. Firstly, that the police primarily collect the evidence means that contamination can occur, affecting the results of forensic tests. If items of clothing from a victim and a suspect are placed together at any time during an investigation, obviously DNA from the suspect's clothing will be found on that belonging to the victim. Without the availability of quality university courses and rigorous training, no standards are set by which competence in the field of forensic science can be measured. As a result, too many people are operating as scientists, offering their services to the courts, without the skills and experience required to do the job properly.

The FSS was established as an executive agency of the Home Office in April 1991. In April 1996, it was merged with the Metropolitan Police Forensic Science Laboratory, making it by far the largest supplier of forensic science services in the UK. In 1999 the FSS was given trading fund status, which allows it to retain surplus cash at the end of each financial year and carry it over to the next, naturally to be spent on improving the service to customers. It now offers services to private, public and overseas customers as well as the forty-three police forces in England and Wales, the CPS and HM Customs and Excise.

The purpose of the FSS is to

...serve the administration of justice principally by providing scientific support in the investigation of crime and expert evidence to the courts.

It aims to do so with

...efficiency, effectiveness and economy.

The three 'Es', as used by the Attorney General in defining a reformed system of disclosure of evidence, sit uncomfortably within the mission statement of the FSS. Statisticians in Austin, Texas, demonstrated that 1 in every 100 forensic tests performed on the DNA of suspected criminals might give a false result. Jonathan Koehler, a teaching professor at the University of Texas, discovered that human errors occurred during proficiency testing, when laboratories falsely matched samples or failed to notice a match during the analysis of a series of known DNA samples. Yet the FSS in Britain examines over half a million items in around 100,000 cases every year and attends 1,200 crime scenes, providing expert evidence in court about 2,500 times each year.

I decided to ask Koehler just how much of an impressive aid he believed DNA to be in identifying criminals or clearing suspects. He told me,

While DNA is indeed a powerful tool, it is important to bear in mind that there is often a large subjective component associated with it. In some cases (though not all or even most), whether samples 'match' or not may depend on something as subjective as one's theory of the case.

As if sensing my confusion he continued,

The point is illustrated nicely in a US case that Professor William Thompson (University of California at Irvine) presented in my law school course a few weeks ago. He showed that in an actual violent crime in which a mixed blood sample was recovered, if one's theory of the case was that there were three contributors (e.g. a victim and two perpetrators), the target suspect 'matched.' But if one's theory of the case was that there were two contributors, this same suspect was excluded. This ambiguous result may surprise people who think that one either does or doesn't match a DNA profile.

It certainly surprised me. My mind boggled with the possibilities, mainly that DNA evidence sounded more like a hypothesis at times, made up of opinions and ideas rather than fact.

In its targets for 2002–03 the FSS aims to achieve a ten per cent return on capital employed and a ten per cent efficiency gain. In terms of its service delivery it aims to speed up turnaround time for completed casework. That the report places financial objectives before service delivery targets is perhaps worrying, but worse is that nowhere in its report does the FSS show concern about or even acknowledge rates of error. To the contrary, Chris Hadkiss, manager of the DNA laboratory at the FSS, refuses to admit that errors committed by the FSS reach the courtroom. He emphatically stated to enquiring journalist Nick Patton Walsh,

> People make mistakes – no one is disputing that – but we have a quality system here. The mistakes are not allowed to go to court.[5]

Surely he was right. 'Experts' are people with 'special' knowledge and skills after all. They'd be accustomed to the concept of something so basic as *errors* and make provisions for them. Maybe they just didn't bother making mention of them in their annual report because the thought of *nearly* sending innocent people to jail was an instant turn-off. Not exactly something to cheer about. I compared forensic experts to people like lab techs that analyse blood or urine for disease. Occasionally they got it wrong and recalled everyone either to retest them or admit they'd made a mistake. A friend of mine had to live with the 'fact' that he'd got diabetes – for a week – before being told there'd been a mistake and he was fine. It'd been a bummer of a week but at least he hadn't spent it in jail.

Then I discovered that a false DNA match might be the only piece of dodgy evidence to reach the courtroom where people who often didn't know any better then translated it into proof. Thank life for the solicitors, albeit few and far between, with the initiative to challenge evidence of this kind, before it gets that far.

Raymond Easton was arrested in April 1999, charged with committing a burglary in Bolton, over 200 miles away from where he lived. Electrical equipment, to the value of £440, had been stolen. A spot of blood had been found on a broken window at the crime scene and police claimed that it matched Easton's DNA. His DNA was held on the national database following a domestic incident in 1995, when he had received a caution. He was picked up and jailed by Swindon Police, on behalf of Greater Manchester Police.

It did not worry the police in the slightest that Easton suffered from advanced Parkinson's Disease, could not dress himself nor drive and lived over 200 miles away from the crime scene. In addition he had a strong alibi and claimed he'd been looking after a sick daughter at home, as many family members would also confirm. Police in Manchester could not identify any possible suspects in the case and so had performed a 'cold hit' on the DNA database, trawling through it until they found a match by chance.

Due to his solicitor demanding further, more sophisticated DNA tests, Easton was exonerated and the charge against him was dropped months later. The retest was carried out on a ten-point testing system called SGM Plus, rather than the six-point DNA testing system as had been tested originally. The additional four loci did not match Easton's DNA and so the tests were proved false.[6]

It was said that the chances of a false match occurring were 1 in 37,000,000. Many mathematicians, however, are sure such events are actually routine occurrences that happen all the time. They insist that presenting such calculations in this way to a court is to mislead the jury deliberately. In Britain this was standard practice until shortly after this case was exposed and the FSS started to upgrade its testing and database to SGM Plus ten-point scales.

Mr Easton was lucky. Although he was forced to spend time in prison, thanks to a competent solicitor his case never got to court. Robert Watters was not so fortunate.[7] In October 1999 he was convicted in Birmingham Crown Court, before a jury, on four counts of burglary and was sentenced to a total of six years' imprisonment. The only evidence linking him to the burglaries consisted of DNA taken from cigarette ends found at one crime scene, which allegedly matched seven regions of his own DNA. Because the robberies shared certain features that made them all very similar, the police were able to charge Watters with all four.

In the opinion of Ms Tomlinson, a forensic expert, the probability of a false match in this kind of situation, based on the assumption that the appellant had no close relatives (he had two brothers), was 1 in 86,000,000. If Watters had two brothers then the probability of a false match increased to 1 in 267. She agreed that the results did not mean that the cellular material actually did come from Watters and also stated that DNA evidence should not be used in isolation and without other supporting evidence.

The prosecution had no other evidence to support their case but added that Watters was a smoker, lived in the area in which the burglaries took place and was also male, the inference being that most safe crackers were male. Unwittingly supporting this daft crown case, the judge allowed the jury to exclude the brothers from possible involvement. Police officers had not investigated either of the brothers so in actual fact they were in no way excluded from possible involvement.

But let's ignore for the moment the fact that the police may have caught the wrong brother and consider the odds given, if the brothers could have been excluded from involvement through fantastic police work – a 1 in 37,000,000 chance that the match may be false.

When applying the product rule, the forensic scientist assumes that no two people in the target population are related and that all opposite gender members of the population are equally likely to mate with each other and produce offspring. This means that the DNA database needs to be large enough and random enough to reflect the distribution of people in a population. How precise can a database be that is made up of people disproportionately from certain ethnicities and geographical areas? Such data cannot be equated to a random sample of the British population.

Michael Strutt, a researcher and spokesman for Justice Action in New South Wales, Australia, explains that forensic experts attempt to reflect the lack of precision in DNA databases by calculating *confidence levels*.[8] These are numeric levels that attempt to quantify the 'typicalness' of the samples used in the database (i.e. the confidence that they are representative samples of the target population as a whole). Confidence limits are often not mentioned in court because match odds of, say, 37,000,000 to 1 bear no relationship to the *real* possibility of a match by chance. *Likelihood ratios* are another way of presenting DNA match odds and are commonly used in court, perhaps because they don't represent the *real* possibility of a match by chance. They are calculated with no consideration of factors such as close relatives, inbred populations or the size of the database.

In the case of Easton, the forensic expert failed to mention that there was about a sixty per cent chance that *at least* one other person in the entire UK would have matched the crime stain recovered from the crime scene. There was also about *one chance in fifty-three* that at least one other person on the FSS database would have matched it, according to the test applied. In other words, based on the size of the database (which contained about 700,000 personal profiles at the time), a match would have been made in about one of every fifty-three profiles examined against it.

Add to this the possibility of mislabelling or mixing up the results, or procedural errors caused by the materials being used to test the sample such as chemicals, machinery or software. Crime stains are rarely of optimum size and contain inorganic matter that can interfere with testing. Stains can also be degraded over time and via microbial activity, or mixed with DNA from other human and non-human sources. Given all these factors, it's possible that the result would have thrown up a match by error.

In the case of Watters, he spent a year in prison and was released in October 2000 after having an appeal allowed. The judge conceded that he should never have been convicted and that such flimsy evidence should not have gone to the jury. But it did.

Britain has a population of 58,000,000 people, and according to Michael Strutt, looking for cold hits in the absence of other evidence effectively makes everyone a suspect, whether on the database or not. Even with match odds of the order of millions to one there is a significant chance that the wrong person may be matched to the sample. Police defend their actions by claiming that it is more than likely that a suspect found by matching to the database will be a repeat offender. Such prejudiced opinions result in many ex-prisoners protesting their innocence, though they are rarely listened to.

Michael Strutt believes that it will probably take a publicised false match against a prominent and respectable person before the unreliability of database trawling for suspect-less 'cold hits' becomes widely recognised. Until this happens he is certain innocent people will continue to be linked to crime scenes via false matches on DNA databases. In fact he is sure (based on statistical analysis that he has carried out) that there are already innocent people in British prisons due to matches by chance during database trawls.

Koehler advised,

> The best way we can learn about the rates at which false positive (and false negative) errors are committed by laboratory analysts is to provide the analysts with blind, external proficiency tests. Because such tests are rare in practice we don't have an accurate sense of error rates for DNA technologies (or most other forensic science technologies, for that matter).

I wondered why an organisation such as the FSS would choose not to make damn good use of proficiency testing if it was such a good thing and turned again to Michael Strutt. He replied,

> The lab accreditation regime in the UK calls for such proficiency testing but the results have not been publicly available since the mid-1990s. This is due to 'commercial in confidence' provisions and increasing hostility from the forensic science community towards anything which might provide a quantitative estimate of the chance that a test has been messed up.

He went on to explain,

> There are widely accepted mathematical methods such as Bayes' Theorem. These can be used to combine the estimate of a 'match by chance' obtained from a statistical database with the estimate of a 'match by error' obtained from the results of proficiency testing the technician which did the testing. Doing so would produce match odds far less impressive than those routinely thrown around courtrooms and used to sell forensic DNA testing to the public.

People throughout the world have come to regard fingerprint identification as infallible too, and it is this gullible attitude that has brought about the destruction of more innocent lives. The standard and competence of fingerprint experts in Scotland leaves much to be desired, with the Scottish Criminal Record Office (SCRO) seeming to operate on little more than pot luck and a huge helping of arrogance on occasion.

In 1997, Marion Ross, a middle-aged woman from Kilmarnock, was brutally murdered in her home and Detective Constable Shirley McKie was assigned to the case.[9] During the initial investigation fingerprints were lifted from the house. However, when these were brought to the SCRO for analysis, an expert matched one of the prints to that of McKie. The examiner claimed to have matched sixteen points of a print to her left thumbprint. Three other examiners checked this identification and clarified that it was indeed her print. Shirley was astounded, insisting that she had never stepped inside the house.

Nobody believed her, and even her father, himself a former superintendent, initially found it difficult to believe that the experts could get it wrong.[10] In the eyes of the police, fingerprint evidence was infallible. They figured she must have been in the house at some point, had contaminated the crime scene and was lying about it. The more Shirley insisted that she had never been inside the house, the more people began to question her sanity, finding it easier to believe that she was going crazy if not lying. She was even offered a job transfer if only she would admit that she had temporarily lost her mind.

Another fingerprint identified at the scene of the crime was alleged to belong to a man called David Asbury. After police searched his house they took a biscuit tin containing £1,800 and claimed a print on the tin belonged to Marion Ross, the murder victim. He was arrested and charged with the murder. Shirley was called to give evidence at the trial and explain why her print was present at the crime scene. Terrified, Shirley repeated in court that she had never before stepped inside the house. David Asbury was convicted of murder and sentenced to life imprisonment. Months later, Shirley's police force arrested her. She was charged with perjury and suspended from her job.

Feeling alone and completely at a loss, Shirley contemplated suicide. The idea of being found guilty of something she hadn't done was appalling, and members of her own police force treating her with hostility began to take its toll. Her father, realising that it was fingerprints that linked the murder suspect to the crime, was forced to face up to his prejudices as a former policeman. For a hundred years the police had deemed fingerprint identifications concrete proof of guilt. Believing in his daughter and supporting her claims of innocence, he had to be prepared to challenge the evidence. He began to believe that pressure on the police to get a conviction had led to Strathclyde Police fabricating evidence or the SCRO misidentifying the print.

Shirley and her father contacted Pat Wertheim, head of the fingerprint bureau at the Los Angeles Police Department, asking him to fly to Scotland to study the print. He agreed, and after looking at the evidence with a colleague, David Grieve, concluded that the print was not fabricated – it simply wasn't her print. He found it difficult to digest the fact that not one but four fingerprint experts at the SCRO had managed to misidentify the print.

At the High Court, the jury took less than an hour to reach their verdict. In 1999 Shirley McKie was found not guilty of perjury and the identification was overturned in court in the first ever trial to challenge successfully fingerprint identification and win. But this was not an event that was to mark the end of her ordeal. Police officers continued to be antagonistic towards McKie, going so far as to tell newspaper journalists that she was far from innocent, and that Pat Wertheim could not be trusted as a fingerprint expert, while the SCRO maintained that their experts had made a correct identification.

BBC investigative reporter Shelley Jofre, preparing a television programme about the case, invited five more independent experts to check the identification. All five agreed that the print definitely did not match that of McKie. Jofre then decided to ask two of the experts to examine the print that allegedly belonged to Marion Ross, on the biscuit tin taken from David Asbury, who'd been convicted of her murder. They concluded that the print match was also false. Ironically, it was the same four experts at the SCRO that had matched Ross's print.

After Shelley Jofre broke the news in Scotland, a government inquiry into the SCRO was set up, calling for a total overhaul of the fingerprint organisation and making as many as twenty-eight recommendations for change. The four experts involved were suspended from duty (on full pay) while the SCRO carried out its own investigation. The Crown Office in Scotland allowed David Asbury an appeal and he was released from prison in August 2000. In August 2002 his murder conviction was quashed. In March 2002, five years after McKie's ordeal began, the SCRO had the audacity to conclude in an internal report that,

> No matters of misconduct or lack of capability have taken place in the work surrounding the fingerprint comparisons of the McKie and Asbury marks and prints.

The McKie family were advised that no other information would be made available and the report would not be published. With its blatant lack of transparency the four experts returned to work and the SCRO succeeded in completely exonerating itself from any wrongdoing. According to the SCRO, no one was responsible for erroneous fingerprint identifications and no disciplinary action would be taken. It was of no significance to them that an innocent man had been sentenced to life imprisonment or that McKie's career as a police officer was over and that she'd been reduced to a nervous wreck by her treatment. Instead, the report stated that fingerprint evidence was a matter of opinion, not fact, and as such, the SCRO had done nothing wrong.

The family contacted reporter Shelley Jofre to inform her of the report. Jofre called up Chief Constable Andrew Brown of the SCRO to discuss the matter further.

He stated, 'These are opinions of experts and in this particular case they differ.'

Jofre was not convinced. 'So are you saying that the print belonged to McKie or not?'

Brown hesitated. 'A difference of opinion occurred and the correct decision was made in court. A whole range of processes have since been put in place.'

Jofre continued, 'But as long as you talk about a difference of opinion you allow the public to think that oh well, it just depends on which expert you believe.'

Brown replied, 'No, it doesn't depend on which experts you believe.'

Jofre could not get much more out of him to clear up the situation. Instead international experts from around the world were invited to examine the fingerprint evidence once again, and 159 experts declared that there was no way the print could be identified as belonging to Shirley McKie.

Allan Bayle, one of Britain's leading fingerprint scientists working for the Metropolitan Police, and with twenty-five years' experience in the field, was outraged by the SCRO internal report. In a memo he scathingly wrote,

> Welcome to the police state of Scotland. The SCRO is right and everybody else is wrong. It's pure fantasy. The fingerprint community should ban all links with the SCRO until they admit to their mistakes. What a travesty of justice.

Iain McKie, Shirley's father, also remains adamant that the SCRO should admit to their wrongdoing. He recently reiterated the family's position in continuing their fight for justice.

> The relevant marks either belong to Shirley McKie and Marion Ross or they don't. If they don't, and the overwhelming bulk of evidence points to this, then the SCRO experts are either incompetent or criminal.

Shirley has sued the Scottish Executive for civil compensation for the loss of her career and the trauma suffered over nearly six years. To date their lawyers refuse to admit responsibility and it may yet go to a civil hearing. The agony continues.

I find it amazing, even as I'm surrounded daily by images of British and American fighter jets dropping bombs all over Iraq. We're all entitled to differences of opinion when it comes to religion or politics, but when it comes to presenting evidence to a court where you may get locked up, you would think that the process consisted of more than just a paid-for opinion to match your claims. Strathclyde Police had no qualms when it came to charging McKie with perjury. It seems odd that no one is prepared to dismiss the SCRO experts for incompetence. According to Pat Wertheim,

> For the SCRO to try and justify their errant fingerprint 'experts' ' actions with the explanation that fingerprint identification is simply a matter of opinion is to make a mockery of the whole realm of forensic science.

On 5 October 1999 Alan McNamara was arrested by Greater Manchester Police and charged with a £30,000 burglary in Rochdale.[11] He was charged on the basis of a single thumbprint, allegedly found on a jewellery case at the scene of the crime. He had no motive to steal because he owned a discount store that made a profit of £100,000 the year of the burglary and has always claimed that he is innocent. No other evidence linked him to the crime.

Terence Burchell, the crime-scene examiner for Greater Manchester Police contradicted the evidence in his witness statement. While the owners of the house stated that the jewellery box was clean, he had described it as being dirty and sticky. The owners also said that the burglar had left behind a dirty footprint on their bed and tool marks on the windows. Burchell failed to mention any of this in his statement, nor did he take any photographs of the prints, as recommended in Home Office guidelines.

The McNamara family called upon two independent fingerprint experts to check the identification, convinced the police had made a mistake. Both Pat Wertheim and Allan Bayle checked the print and agreed that the thumbprint belonged to McNamara. However, it could not have come from the jewellery case because wood grain would have to show up on the print as a textured surface.

The police remained adamant that they had charged the right person and when questioned about the lack of a textured surface on the print they'd taken, replied that this was down to the examiner's lifting technique. Pat Wertheim, somewhat taken aback, explained that no fingerprint expert in the world was aware of a technique for lifting a print from a textured surface so that the texturing did not show up on it. He said,

> It's impossible under any known technique anywhere in the world. If Greater Manchester Police have developed such a technique then they failed to publish it, or get it peer reviewed or even have it examined by any other expert outside of their agency.

Allan Bayle agreed conclusively that the thumbprint could not have come from the jewellery box in question. He was adamant that the print must have been lifted from a curved, smooth object like a vase, suggested by the creases on the tape and the shape of the print. The police experts then claimed that the box was dirty when the lift was taken, which was why the wood grain hadn't shown up on the lift.

On 25 June 2001 Alan McNamara was found guilty of the burglary by all twelve jurors. Pat Wertheim was shocked.

> Never in my wildest imagination did I think that a jury could convict with no evidence whatsoever except one single thumbprint, which in itself was flawed.

He added defiantly,

> I know I'll be criticised for speaking out against the system like this, but I'm staking my reputation on this case and I know I'm right.

Allan Bayle's career as a fingerprint expert for the Metropolitan Police spanned twenty-five years and once he discovered that McNamara owned a discount store and sold hundreds of vases every year, the case seemed totally improbable. When Scotland Yard refused to let Bayle provide expert witness for McNamara he resigned, determined to speak out.

It was not enough to clear McNamara, who received a sentence of two and a half years, of which he served over a year before being released on 19 August 2002. The family are sure that his print came from a vase or some similar shaped object that Alan had touched quite innocently in his shop or in one of his supplier's warehouses.

Bayle remains convinced that an injustice has taken

place. He continues to assist McNamara in his fight to clear his name and has conducted experiments on the jewellery box, dirtying it with a variety of substances, from makeup to household cleaners. No matter what he puts on the box, when taking a print off it, the wooden texture of the box still shows up on the lift. It is interesting to note that the police force that arrested McNamara is the same force that wrongly charged Raymond Easton.

---

1 *The Times*, 25 July 2000, *The Guardian*, 4 May 1999.

2 Plotnikoff, J., Woolfson, R., 'A fair balance? Evaluation of the operation of disclosure law' (RDS Occasional Paper No 76, RDS Directorate, Home Office, 2001).

3 Forensic Science Service, www.forensic.gov.uk.

4 Callan, K., *Kevin Callan's Story: A Convicted Man's Tireless Campaign for Freedom and Truth* (Warner Books, 1998).

5 *The Observer*, 2 February 2002.

6 Article by Strutt, M., found at http://home.iprimus.com.au/dna_info/dna/.

7 Moenssens, A. A., editor of www.forensic-evidence.com, an information centre in forensic science, law and public policy for lawyers, forensic scientists, educators and public officials.

8 Interview with the author.

9 *Panorama*, 'Finger of Suspicion', BBC 1, 8 July 2001; *Panorama*, 'Fingerprints on Trial', BBC 1, 19 May 2002.

10 Conversation with the author.

11 *Panorama*, op cit. Also based on conversation with the author.

3

How Miscarriages of Justice are Perpetuated in the System

Once we are aware of just how easy it is to become the next victim of a miscarriage of justice, it becomes necessary to find out how easy it is to channel the merits of your case back to a judge and jury, who can then make an informed decision on whether or not to quash your case and have you released.

If you are innocent of the crime of which you have been convicted, it is possible that someone working within the criminal justice system will know it, as well as people closely associated with the crime itself, such as witnesses and the actual perpetrator(s). To begin with it will be extremely difficult to obtain the evidence required to prove your innocence from a prison cell. Prison is after all meant to house the guilty. Once branded and stigmatised, why should a whole justice system made up of the most elite institutions, the very fabric of society, supposedly there to protect the innocent and convict the guilty, be willing to accept fallibility on the claims of a lowly, banished prisoner? The longer you spend in jail, the more stale your case becomes and the more difficult it gets to find the evidence that would clear you. It's your word among thousands of other prisoners against the might of the state.

From this perspective alone, a person alleging to have suffered a miscarriage of justice is truly up against the odds to prove it. The CCRC is solely responsible for investigating alleged miscarriages of justice and no one else, in theory, should need to intervene or make a fuss. However, it has been in operation since 1997 and thousands of people are still languishing in jail, having denied guilt for over twenty years.

Those responsible for putting innocent people into jail do so for a number of reasons. In the case of the Birmingham Six, government agencies and the police were under immense pressure to find and convict the people responsible for the planting of the Birmingham IRA bombs. They felt so much pressure that they must have decided anyone would do. It became more important to charge and convict as quickly as possible than to worry about the real perpetrators or the safety of the nation. Justice was seen to be done when in reality one of the biggest injustices in recent British history was unfolding.

———————

Stephen Hector was sentenced to life in June 1998 for murder. He sent a letter to MOJO in January 2002 from the A Wing at HMP Wakefield:

On the 19th June I was sentenced to life for murder. On the 20th June I sat in my cell and wrote a letter to Mr Copsey, my case solicitor at the time of my trial.

In my letter I asked him to go through my case papers and

sort out a list of them for me. He was to do one of two things once he had got these papers for me and that was either to bring them up on a visit and hand them over or if that wasn't possible he was to send them in to me. Here is the list of papers that I asked him for:

1 All of the written notes by Mr John Murphy.
2 All of my written correspondence that I had either sent to or handed to him between the 9th October 1997 to the 8th June 1998.
3 All of my personal letters to him from the 9th October 1997 through to the present day.
4 All of the transcripts from the summing up of the trial i.e. the trial judge's comments, the defence closing speech and the prosecution closing speech, etc.
5 The report done for the prosecution psychiatrist, Dr Joseph.
6 All of the written correspondence from Mr Copsey to my case barrister regarding my trial and the way they intended to run it.

Not long after I had sent this letter, Mr Copsey arranged to come and visit me. On the visit he gave me a form and asked me to sign it. I asked him what the form was about as I am dyslexic and find it hard to read and write. He replied that the form was routine procedure and that it was only to say that the firm that he worked for would hold my case papers for five years.

I again asked Mr Copsey about the list of papers and he advised me that until the Legal Aid Board had paid everyone, he would be unable to release my papers to me. I asked him when that would be and he advised me that he would write to me and let me know. He then asked why I wanted this list of papers and I told him that it was because I felt I had been left in the dark during my trial. Also from the information that I had received from my friends and family, who had sat through the trial, the information that was put to the jury was not what I had said during my meetings with Mr Copsey. It was in fact the opposite of what I had told him and things were not fully explained to me.

At this point Mr Copsey got up and told me that he had just remembered that he had to go and see another client. He informed me that he would send me a copy of the policy and write to me and let me know about my papers, which he never did. This visit took place at HMP Brixton and that was before the 28th June 1998.

This was the first and last time I ever saw Mr Copsey after my trial. He never sent me the policy nor did he ever send me the papers that I had asked for. Every time that I wrote to him to ask him about my papers he failed to reply.

At the beginning of December 1998 I called his office. When I asked to speak to him his secretary informed me that he wasn't in. This did not come as much of a surprise as I had called on a number of different occasions only to be told the same thing. I asked if she knew if the Legal Aid Board had paid Mr Copsey's fees and she told me she didn't know. I again asked about the case papers and she put me through to Mr John Murphy who asked me if he could help.

I explained the situation to him and he told me he didn't know anything about it. He informed me that he would speak to Mr Copsey and remind him about the policy and the case papers that I had asked for. He also told me that Mr Copsey had misinformed me about the length of time that the firm would hold onto my papers. He informed me that the firm would hold on to them for six years and not five as I had been told. I then explained to Mr Murphy that I still hadn't received a reply to my letters and he assured me that he would raise the matter.

This was the first and last time I spoke to Mr Murphy. In January 1999 I again called the office and asked to speak to Mr Copsey and again I was told that he wasn't there. I again asked the secretary about my papers and again I was told that Mr Copsey hadn't been paid for his services and that as soon as he had he would be in touch with me.

In February 1999 I contacted the Legal Aid Board and asked why Mr Copsey hadn't been paid for his services. I was informed that Mr Copsey had been paid in full for his services. I then explained about the problems that I was having and the reasons he was giving me about holding my case papers back. I was told that Mr Copsey had been paid in full in November 1998. I was also told that I was entitled to all of the paperwork and that Mr Copsey could not hold onto it.

In March 1999 I again wrote to Mr Copsey at his office enquiring about my paperwork. I also told him that I had made enquiries and was fully aware that he had been paid and had no right to withhold my papers from me. I again submitted a list of the paperwork that I wanted and sent it with my letter. I never got a reply nor did I receive any of my paperwork.

I finally got a letter from Mr Copsey on 24th September 1999 and the tone of the letter basically told me to quit asking for the paperwork and just to get on with my sentence. I did not receive any other letter from Mr Copsey after that date – nor did I receive the paperwork that I had been asking for since June 1998.

In December 1999 I wrote to Mr Copsey and advised him that I was going to be transferred from HMP Brixton to HMP Wakefield on the 24th January 2000. I also informed him that once I had sorted myself out in the new prison I would write to him and make some sort of arrangement for a member of my family to come to his office and pick up the paperwork that I had been requesting since 1998.

In February 2000 I again wrote to Mr Copsey informing him that I had been moved and had not received a reply from him. I begged him to write to me with a date when a member of my family could come and pick up the paperwork. I added that the individual would have a letter of authority from me giving him permission to hand over the papers. Once again I didn't hear anything from him. ·

On the 2nd May 2000 I wrote again, saying that the situation was getting out of hand and that the programmes department at HMP Wakefield had asked me to sign a form saying that I was willing to give them permission to obtain my case papers. When I told them that this would be very difficult as my solicitor was refusing to release them to me, they took this as an indication that I was refusing to cooperate with them. They told me that unless I handed over my case papers I wouldn't make any progress through the system and I wouldn't be able to move on from HMP Wakefield.

Again I received no reply from Mr Copsey about this matter. Due to this situation I am now finding it extremely difficult to make any kind of progress within the system. Also because I don't have any kind of paperwork from my defence I am unable to shed any light on what happened to me during the 'offence'. I am also unable to challenge anything that the programmes department say as they have statements from the police and that is all. I am unable to see both sides of the case, or how I came to be involved.

I have tried to explain this to Mr Copsey but as I never get any reply from him I can only assume that he is refusing to help me sort out this situation. The programmes department look upon me as withholding information. This is untrue as I am not sure what happened in my case hence the letters asking for my paperwork.

I think that just about covers everything but if you want any more information please let me know. I had a friend type this out for me as I didn't want to confuse the issue with my dyslexia. He knows about my case and told me that he is willing to type out any further letters for me. I hope that this will help and make it easier for you to read and understand.

From Stephen Hector

For over four years, Stephen Hector has been trying to pick up the threads of the case that resulted in him being convicted of murder. At the time of writing it appears that his case files have been lost or destroyed, as he was eventually informed when he instructed another firm of solicitors to locate the papers. In this position it is impossible for him to draw up any grounds that may lead to a referral to the CA. He is effectively stuck and also has learning difficulties.

The body responsible for handling complaints against solicitors is the Law Society's Office for the Supervision of Solicitors (OSS), and they cannot cope with the number of complaints they receive each year, which, in the past year (2003) rose to over 14,880.[1] If complainants cannot resolve their grievances with the OSS, the matter can be referred to the Legal Services Ombudsman, someone who cannot be a qualified lawyer and who is completely independent of the legal profession.[2]

The remit of the ombudsman includes overseeing the

OSS but serious concerns have been raised year after year, and they seem to be largely unheeded. The ombudsman has the power to recommend that the OSS reconsider complaints and may also recommend that the OSS, or solicitor complained about, pay compensation for loss, distress or inconvenience caused, which is not much help for wrongfully convicted prisoners.

In 2002 the then Legal Services Ombudsman for England and Wales, Ann Abraham, lamented,

> A multiplicity of agencies has produced a regulatory regime which cannot be seen to be operating in the public interest. Sometimes it seems that the OSS create problems for themselves and their customers by neglecting the very basics of complaint handling – like reading the information the complainant sends them.

In 2003 when Zahida Manzoor replaced Abraham, she reported,

> I was particularly struck by how little tangible progress appears to have been made by the professional bodies over the past fifteen years.

By 2001 Abraham had become so dissatisfied with the level of performance of the OSS that she deemed it pointless to set any targets for 2002. She believed that the figure for the OSS's overall work in progress for complaints was 'significantly understated' and that their figures for turnaround times were 'incomplete, unreliable and understated'. Targets for 2001 had included the closure of all complaints cases dating back to 1998. It remains today that the OSS are closing significantly fewer cases than they are receiving and Manzoor has stated that from January 2001, output at the OSS has merely declined dramatically.

In July 2001 the Law Society's Council approved a model for a consumer redress scheme, and shortly after issued a consultation paper outlining their proposals. Although Abraham had expressed a number of concerns about them they were largely ignored. It seems that the Law Society may be another one of these confused, outdated institutions, with members who are reluctant to engage in communication with stakeholders. Manzoor remains doubtful that the scheme will serve to forge either fresh public confidence in the Law Society's complaints-handling service, or the 'swift and appropriate remedies' that have been promised to clients.

Shifting mentally between differing sections of society, certain attitudes permeate and it is only fair to state that personally I am equable by nature. My own view of the law makes me a walking contradiction. On the one hand it's this powerful tool that has been historically used to intimidate and control certain people. High-society white men traditionally formulated it to control everyone else. If you didn't belong to high society, you didn't belong anywhere near the right side of the law. Law equated to subordination. On the other hand, the experiences of grass-roots anti-racist and women's organisations, and the most oppressed individuals (such as those who've been wrongfully imprisoned) have led them to embrace the law as a necessary means of defending themselves from injustice.

If the law is prepared to oppress people, in whatever form, then people must be prepared to challenge it. For the victim of a gross miscarriage of justice, rotting in a cell, it would be crazy not to use the law as a necessary tool to put wrongs right. Even when he or she knows full well that the legal system is an elitist, corrupt system in major crisis, responsible for their wrongful imprisonment in the first place.

Court of Appeal (CA) and Criminal Cases Review Commission (CCRC)

If something goes seriously wrong at your trial, the CA is there to re-examine your case. In the interests of justice the CA should order the production of any evidence connected to the proceedings and the examination of any witness at the trial. In doing so, the court will consider whether the evidence is believable and if it affords grounds for allowing the appeal. This sounds fair enough on the surface.

Under the old law (1968 Criminal Appeal Act until 1995) the CA had a duty to admit fresh evidence where it was not available at the original trial – if they thought it would be in the interests of justice. But the court did not necessarily *have* to submit fresh evidence to a jury and let a jury decide. This approach was criticised by Lord Devlin who argued that it was wrong in principle for judges to decide whether an appellant was guilty or not.[3] Especially when we consider that to the current day our judges are almost exclusively white, male and drawn from upper- or upper-middle-class families who have attended public school and then Oxford or Cambridge.

Nearly all of our judges are over sixty years old and in general, the older they are, the higher their rank.

Pause to consider this. How many white, male judges with their privileged backgrounds can really understand the issues surrounding ghetto violence or domestic violence against women? How can they understand what it is like to be working class or Irish or Palestinian and innocent? Yet if they don't have an understanding of these issues how can we expect them to administer justice properly? If an oppressed woman suffers years of physical and sexual assault and eventually kills her husband in self-defence, in fear of her life, how can we seriously expect a rich, white male who's never been subjected to any violence or dependence in his life, to be able to relate to her state of mind and hence to any psychiatric evidence? If a police officer brutalises a suspect into making a false confession, can we really expect a high-society judge to be capable of realisation?

The simple answer is that *we* cannot because *he* cannot. This is why we conduct trial by jury and not trial by judge, though it seems we are about to lose this right in some circumstances under the new Criminal Justice Bill. Under the old law the CA would regularly uphold convictions, even if there was strong, fresh evidence that cast doubt upon its safety, such as defence lawyers' negligence or non-disclosure of evidence by the police or prosecution.

Under the amended act, if new evidence exists, which *could* have affected the outcome of an original trial, the appeal judges have a duty to put the evidence towards a jury by ordering a retrial. However, according to seasoned miscarriage-of-justice lawyers and campaigners today, many appeal court judges are regularly 'second guessing' jurors again, and upholding convictions in the face of convincing fresh evidence.

Campbell Malone, a highly respected solicitor of Stephensons in Bolton, recently stated,

> Appeal court judges are saying that it is their function to determine whether a conviction is safe or not, even if they have accepted that there is relevant, credible, fresh evidence.[4]

Juries may be far from perfect but they have more in common with the average citizen than a judge. It is attitude that frames a judge's performance and every time he is blind to the reality of a case, he shows he is unfit for the job. Every time a convicted person at the Appeal Court is judged on grounds that have nothing to do with the facts of their case, confidence in the law is lost and injustices are perpetuated.

For almost two years, Hazel Keirle worked on a critical analysis and review of the efficiency of the Criminal Court of Appeal and the CCRC.[5] It was important for her to consider whether a greater proportion of miscarriages of justice could be prevented than currently exists within the system. According to informed public opinion, the CA has again developed an increasing trend of disregard to natural justice in dealing with first-time criminal appeals and those referred back by the commission. Restricting her research to convictions in the crown court following trials by jury, Keirle was to make some astounding discoveries.

In the year 2000, 71,330 cases for trial were disposed of by the crown courts and 2,068 applications for leave to appeal against conviction were made. That is an approximate representation of 2.8 per cent. In the same year 150 convictions were quashed by the CA – an approximate representation of 0.02 per cent of convictions and 7 per cent of applicants for leave to appeal. These statistics indicate that the crown court claims to get it right 99.98 per cent of the time!

In today's carved-up society our judges should surely consider the concept of law and justice for different sections of society. It used to be the north-south divides, but today it's not just white Britain. It's black Britain, Asian Britain, Irish Britain, mixed Britain, women's Britain, youth of Britain, HIV Britain, gay and lesbian Britain – the list goes on. When we add working-, middle- and upper-class Britain, every single one of us can be subdivided into a scattering of the three, according to the job we hold down – or don't, as the case may be. We can stagnate in one section of society or, if by chance rootless and rebellious from an early age, opt to spend our lives roaming with as many sections of society as we can before we die.

Maybe it has everything to do with the old imperial saying, 'divide and rule'. Unless we are willing to cross these barriers with an open mind, the Britain that we all love and care for is in very real and immediate danger of signing its own life-imprisonment warrant by default.

Of those who were convicted and failed at appeal, some will have turned to the CCRC. The CCRC is receiving an average of 520 eligible applications each year and defines itself as

>...an independent body investigating miscarriages of justice,

which

> ...can seek further information relating to a case
> and carry out its own investigations, or arrange
> for others to do so.

In the 2002 annual report, the CCRC also described itself as having wide-ranging investigative powers to secure materials and obtain expert advice. It is accountable to the public through Parliament for its performance. Interestingly, the commission can also

> ...refer cases to the Home Secretary where it feels
> a Royal Pardon should be considered.

I have asked the CCRC to inform me of the criteria necessary for such referrals but am still waiting for a reply.

Five hundred and twenty eligible applications each year represents less than one per cent of crown court convictions and is a persuasive figure, indicating that the majority of applicants to the commission may well have been wrongly convicted. But in 2001 the commission was referring just 3.6 per cent of its completed cases, compared to 19.35 per cent in its first year of operation. Double the staff and a huge increase in the rate of case completions resulted in a far lower percentage of referrals that continues to this day.

When considering levels of efficiency it is pertinent to add that the first chairman, Sir Frederick Crawford, took home an annual salary of £110,000. This was a part-time appointment and he was over seventy years old. Some people might wonder if he could justify his position on any basis other than that he is a freemason. Of the fourteen commission members, there used to be two women who earned the lowest salaries. Fiona King earned £30,000 working part time while the chief executive, Jacky Courtney, took home £10,000 a year on a full-time basis. When they resigned from their posts men replaced them.

In 2001 the commission reviewed 885 cases and made final negative decisions on 853 of them. The commission's expenditure that year was in excess of £5 million. The following year the commission managed to spend in excess of £6 million. Over half of that was spent on employment costs, of which £1 million went straight to the commission members, though they employ over ninety staff. The referral figures were even worse.

According to Keirle,

> Many of the rejected applicants are now seeking help from external organisations and onwards to the legal profession, where they had not had the benefit of competent, experienced representation during the review process.

Other applicants are also trying to apply to the CCRC straight after conviction, which they cannot do. The CCRC can't help those who haven't appealed. By the time they've made an application and the CCRC have written back and said sorry, we can't help you, they've wasted a year. This happens on a regular basis, which demonstrates bad communication skills on the part of the CCRC. So then these people have to go to the CA on their own, and lose. That takes about nine months and then they go back to the CCRC; that'll take up another two years, and then the CCRC will refuse their case, say they've got no grounds anyway and throw them out.

For people like me, Keirle epitomises a guiding light, shining through the mad chaos that makes up the criminal justice system. Directing me to a seemingly endless network of lawyers, journalists, forensic experts, MPs and affected families, I wonder how she does it under the conditions that she works in. Completely overwhelmed with cries for assistance MOJO has nothing like the resources that the CCRC has to work with.

In the CCRC publication *Getting Help With Your Application* it states:

> It is not essential to use a solicitor when applying, but there are real benefits to having your own legal representative.

According to Keirle, fifty per cent of applicants to the CCRC are not legally advised or represented but no unrepresented applicant has *ever* had a referral to the CA. It is next to impossible for the lay client to present his or her case to the commission and identify the criteria necessary.

Keirle's research also revealed that the commission did not appear to conduct any investigation into cases beyond that which appeared on the face of the basic papers. They rarely secured all the appropriate materials and often made no enquiries into original trial solicitors or the defence material that may still lurk in their files. Few commission members visited prisoners or even made detailed enquiries of them, when it should be obvious that the applicant knows his or her case better than anyone else.

Other observations included the fact that the final statement of reasons for rejected applicants very often contained no reasons. It was common practice for the commission to reject an application by simply stating that 'the issue' does not affect the safety of the conviction, without giving detailed reasoning.

What disturbs me the most is the fact that the CCRC currently expends over £6 million a year to refer just thirty-odd cases. Even if, being seriously optimistic, we accepted a margin of error of just 1 per cent as opposed to a negligible 0.02 per cent, the commission would be referring on average 175 more applications a year.

Operating like a brand-new vacuum let loose inside a bank vault it is like watching a bunch of fat cats shuffle papers while dodging the persistent queries of lawyers, journalists and campaigners, or telling them untruths about when final decisions on cases will take place. According to MOJO,

> ...in most cases they operate a closed shop policy on information until the review is completed. They rarely keep applicants or their representatives fully appraised of the review as it progresses. Case Review Managers are not working alongside or in conjunction with the applicants' own representatives. They have isolated and distanced themselves and that has resulted in a total loss of trust and faith by the legal profession in the commission.

The commission considers that,

Whenever there is a real possibility that a

conviction would not be upheld by the CA, it will refer the case.

This is where fantasy justice comes into play. For if the CA seriously believes that justice is dispensed 99.98 per cent of the time, what room does that leave for the commission's referral criteria? Each time the commission refers a case and the conviction is upheld, their reasoning within those judgments will prevent the commission making a referral on similar grounds in the future. Never mind that the safety of the conviction is at issue. The guilt or innocence of the defendant doesn't seem to be relevant to the proceedings.

In direct contrast to its workings, it is interesting to note the content of Jack Straw's management statement for the CCRC. He wrote,

> A discretion which was exclusively for the Home Secretary to exercise is thus now regulated by a set of statutory criteria, removed from political or judicial influence.

Bob Woffinden, an investigative journalist with a history of seeking and checking information on behalf of prisoners alleging miscarriages of justice, is only too aware of the problems faced.

> For all practical purposes, the CA is the sole chance that lawyers have of getting a conviction quashed. Accordingly they will become ever more fastidious in preparing their cases, which will take even longer to come on at Appeal. The time it

takes for cases to get through the queue at the CCRC, then to be investigated, and then to reach the Appeal stage is now reaching six years.[6]

Woffinden argues that legislative changes are needed whereby the CCRC should be able to refer *all* cases where it believes there is

> ...a real possibility that justice may have miscarried, not a real possibility that a conviction will not be upheld by a CA.

He adds,

> The present situation is very grave for those caught up in it; it represents an extraordinary waste of public money and it is fast replicating the logjam that originally led to the setting up of the CCRC.

Keirle estimates that,

> At any one time there is a minimum of 1,500 wrongly convicted prisoners, who will be well over their tariffs, costing the state £37.5 million per year. This is money that would be better expended on crime prevention and society protection.

It can be argued that every conviction that is reversed because it is wrong will save the state money.

Of the cases referred by the CCRC back to the CA, approximately thirty-seven per cent of convictions have been upheld, yet all the cases that are referred are very persuasive. Some lawyers believe that the cases meet the criteria for conviction reversal but the CA deals with them in an intellectually dishonest way. In the recent case of Donald Pendleton, his conviction was upheld by the CA but then overturned by the House of Lords. Many other cases exist where convictions have been upheld in the face of an abundance of doubt. They include that of Samar and Jawad, two Palestinians convicted in relation to the Israeli Embassy bombing in 1994; Eddie Guilfoyle, convicted of murdering his wife and Barry George, convicted of murdering Jill Dando, to name but a few.

As if the present situation was not enough to fuel immense public concern about dysfunctional aspects of our criminal justice system, the CCRC destroys applicants' papers four years after rejecting a case. For a convicted prisoner who has waited six to eight years to gather fresh evidence and present it to the CCRC, this represents yet another devastating blow. New evidence can surface years after the CCRC has rejected a case so it seems somewhat callous to destroy the papers.

---

1 The Law Society, www.lawsoc.org.uk. For a summary of performance for 2002–03 go to: http://www.olso.org/AR2003/03-summary.asp.
2 The Legal Services Ombudsman, www.olso.org.
3 Darbyshire, P., *Nutshells, English Legal System* (Sweet and Maxwell, 1998).
4 *The Lawyer*, 25 July 2001. See also *The Times*, 13 March 2001.
5 Keirle, H., *A Critical Analysis and Review of the Criminal Cases Review Commission and the Criminal Court of Appeal* (MOJO, April 2002). Their website can be found at www.mojo.freehosting.net.
6 *The Times*, 20 February 2001.

4

Parole and the Denial of Guilt

A prison term is punishment in itself for the guilty but for the innocent lifer, it's worse than that because they have no idea when it will end. If you dare to challenge your conviction because you are truly innocent, you may not leave prison until you both admit guilt and stop fighting your case, or prove your innocence from every possible and impossible angle.

Parole is far less likely for those who have been found guilty of murder or acts of terrorism and deny it, no matter how well 'behaved' in every other respect. Even having completed a recommended tariff the same may apply because psychologists and probation officers continue to recommend to the Parole Board that those who deny guilt are 'too high a risk factor' to be suitable for release.

It is a fact that prisoners who deny guilt, who have been labelled as IDOM (in denial of murder) are considered more troublesome than those prisoners who are genuinely guilty of murder. Jo Dobry, a member of the Parole Board, conceded,

> Those who claim to be innocent possibly do make life more difficult for us and we do take as fact that prisoners have been rightfully convicted. It is important to understand that we cannot 'go behind' the conviction. That is the job of the Appeal Courts and the Criminal Cases Review Commission.[1]

In other words, the Parole Board, like everyone else, knows that there are innocent prisoners in the system yet they are paid to respect court decisions and refuse parole anyway. There are currently 1,500 lifers in England and Wales who have served past their tariffs, but it is not known how many of those are in denial of guilt.

In order to be eligible for parole consideration, prisoners must be located in Category C prisons. Category A consists of the maximum-security units where prisoners, once convicted of the most serious of crimes, are allocated. The idea is that they progress through the system to Category B, then C, then on to Category D or open conditions in preparation for release, according to the length of tariff received.

In my experience there is little difference between Category A and Category B in terms of making progress through the system. Both consist of hideously overcrowded institutions that mask from the public cruelty, neglect and brutality, while grooming all prisoners to an unprecedented level of professional criminality through mixing with the worst offenders. Satpal Ram as a prisoner bounced back and forth through A and B prisons for the best part of fifteen years. But in order to progress from Category B to C, prison officers will demand that convicts show some degree of remorse. If they refuse, there is no point in letting them be considered for parole.

In order to show remorse, prisoners are expected to confess. They then get the opportunity of being transferred to a prison that carries out offence-related behaviour courses. These are courses that get the convict to address all aspects of the offence and include sex offenders' treatment programmes, anger management and enhanced thinking courses. If successful, the convict gets considered for Category C.

If innocent, how many of us would falsify our guilt to get through the system and back home with family? Telling lies in order to get out of prison does work and Paddy Hill insists,

> ...the guilty are rushed through the system. It may sound funny but that's the truth. Deny guilt and you will languish indefinitely in Category A. But if you're guilty? It's a breeze. You can rape and murder someone, spend a few years attending weird sex treatment courses and tell everyone you're 'cured' and then you're free to go and do it again.

I tried to imagine it – being convicted of a vicious murder and, in truth, not knowing anything about it. You tell the truth in court (as much as you're allowed to) and get convicted. Then you're expected somehow to bow down and tell every conceivable dirty, filthy lie in prison to be considered for parole. All along you know you did nothing wrong, and the weeks slowly turn into months and then years, as your family try to escape the stigma that's suddenly attached to them.

If you were to make a false admission of guilt, who would then be willing to help you prove your innocence by reinvestigating your case? The fact is you would be labelled a murderer for the rest of your life and would only be released on licence, if you were lucky, and with conditions attached.

It is 2004 and the Parole Board still refuses to consider that a convict might be innocent and that parole conditions may hamper their release. In practice, only a small proportion of prisoners maintain their innocence beyond their first few years in prison. There is nothing to be gained from it except a longer sentence and such resistance requires enormous mental strength and endurance.

Prison officers are reputed to use various methods for those who attempt to resist the system in any small way. Prisoners I have spoken to insist that one common tactic is for an officer to stand on a prisoner's neck until he believes he is on the verge of suffocation.[2]

> At the last minute the pressure is released and the prisoner is permitted to breathe. Sometimes this is repeated several times. Not infrequently the officers misjudge and prisoners pass out. In the case of prisoners with asthma the risk of death is significant.

Even prison officers themselves have told of instances where prisoners have been beaten black and blue on the orders of the adjudicating governor for refusing to plead guilty in adjudication. Other forms of brutality include placing prisoners' hands or faces on heated hotplates;

squeezing genitals; placing prisoners in straitjackets with wet towels shoved up the back and leaving them face down in a pool of urine. Complainants are often beaten or intimidated into withdrawing allegations of brutality. Abuses began to receive public attention in the 1990s when the removal of crown immunity meant that prisoners could sue the prison service – however, legal aid has now been removed for such cases and few lawyers are willing to take them on a 'no win, no fee' basis.

To assess a prisoner for parole, parole clerks use reports compiled by prison officers during offence-related behaviour courses. It seems no one at the Parole Board or indeed anywhere else is too bothered about making provisions for those prisoners who refuse to acknowledge their crimes, because they insist they are innocent. Instead prisoners are shown no sympathy and are refused parole time and time again.

Defending the Parole Board, Jo Dobry recently stated,

> Legal precedent established that it would be unlawful for the Board to refuse parole solely on the grounds of denial of guilt or anything that flows from that. The board also takes into account the circumstances in which the crime was committed, and the circumstances and behaviour of the individual prisoner before and during the sentence.

In reality those very few people who are granted parole, having consistently denied guilt, tend to be those who have built up a massive degree of public support over time, sustained by an international campaign, very experienced human-rights lawyers and media support, over a period of years. The Parole Board routinely reject about sixty per cent of those who are eligible for parole, whether guilty or not.

In 1999 the National Audit Office reported that

> In 96% of a sample of rejected applicants, the reasons given for the decision included the prisoner's failure to address offending behaviour.[3]

It also stated,

> Most parole clerks have difficulties in obtaining parole reports from the police and the courts. Lack of cooperation between the different agencies has led to parole clerks carrying out their responsibilities without important information.

In addition, the report stated that two-thirds of parole clerks received no training in parole procedures. Serious delays in processing a prisoner's application for parole continue to be caused by their sudden transfer to another prison during the parole process. Transfers accounted for nearly half of cancelled interviews in 1999. The prison service did not bother to monitor or justify these transfers and the National Audit Office also reported that the estimated cost to the prison service of delays in releasing UK nationals was some £2 million.

When I asked Paddy about measures that could be taken to address the problems of parole for victims of injustice who should be eligible, he replied,

One of the sensible things that Blunkett should do to ease overcrowding in prisons is to review properly and release all the people who are known as IDOMs in jail, and who are over their tariffs. The reason that some of them are not being released is simply because they're in denial and always have been. Yet it's not as if they suddenly jumped on the bandwagon. People like Rob Brown and Paul Blackburn have been asserting their innocence from the *very beginning*. The way they were treating us from so many years ago... it's absolutely shocking. If they *were* guilty they would have been released ten or twelve years ago.

The number of people imprisoned in Britain has now reached over 74,000 for the first time. The prisons were built to house 66,000 people. Prisons chief Martin Narey announced in July 2002 that he had been forced to use police cells for the first time since 1995. Could it be that innocent people are blocking up the system?

Media Support

By the time the Birmingham Six convictions were eventually overturned in March 1991, pressure on the courts had reached an all-time high. The Runciman Commission was underway and the outcry that followed the release of other publicly supported miscarriage cases demonstrated how deeply sceptical the public had become towards a system that was clearly failing people. These cases received a great deal of media attention and figures show a steady increase in the number of appeals being allowed from 1991 to 1993.[4]

After 1993, until 1995, when media interest in the topic of miscarriages had waned, there was a gradual decline in the number of appeals being allowed, but once the CCRC came into being media coverage of disputed cases rose again and there was an increase in the number of appeals being allowed. From June 1998 onwards there has been a steady decline in the number of appeals being allowed. It seems likely that this can be attributed in part to a decrease in the coverage of cases alleging miscarriages of justice.[5]

Before one can point the finger at journalists, however, it is worth mentioning that there are a number of obstacles that exist to deter the investigative journalist from making meaningful enquiries. Until a High Court judgement in 1996 the prison service regularly refused permission for access to prisoners unless journalists signed an agreement that any information gained from the visit would not be used for professional purposes. Today the prison service still attempts to deter journalists.

Simon Hattenstone, a features writer for the *Guardian* newspaper, contacted the prison service in September 2000 with a view to gaining permission to visit Satpal Ram. He was advised that any prisoner appealing against conviction was entitled to one visit from the media but that Ram would prefer to be visited by *Panorama*. So Hattenstone wrote directly to Ram who replied, stating that he would very much like Hattenstone to visit, suggesting he do so as a friend. He included a visiting order with his letter and they were able to meet. A month later the prison service (oblivious to the fact that they had already met), wrote to Hattenstone asking him to explain why he could not resolve any queries he had through written correspondence with the prisoner. They had sent Ram a form in which he was asked to state his preferred media outlet and Ram insisted he'd filled it in stating the *Guardian*, straightaway.

Others attempting to cooperate with the prison service have had to deal with visiting orders being repeatedly 'lost' in the mail or travel hundreds of miles to a prison in anticipation of a booked visit only to find out that the prisoner has suddenly been transferred elsewhere.

The printing of domestic news was illegal in England until the 1640s when limited news items first began to appear on the streets of London. It was illegal because governors were of the view that a 'liberty of discourse' or too much information would undermine the nature of 'proper government'.

The mechanisms used to enforce censorship in England started to break down in the 1640s after the Scottish and Irish rebellions took place. Conflicting political forces led to a division of policy on printing rights between the king and the Houses of Parliament. In short, no single entity could control the press and this led to an increase in the number of unlicensed news-related articles being published. The news pamphlets printed were cheap and quickly drafted, which meant that they were more widely available to different social groups and were no longer just for the privileged. Being unlicensed, new and often controversial issues could be included.[6]

A dramatic increase in the distribution of information fuelled an increase in the political conscience of society. Conflicts between news pamphlets encouraged readers to side on certain issues. The king took advantage by printing propaganda and imprisoning anyone that explicitly attacked his personal integrity.

Since inception the media has been criticised for printing inaccurate, sensationalist and irresponsible reports and its history is strewn with scandals, political bias, and the payment and acceptance of political bribes. Sadly, too many journalists still lack credibility and fair balance today. Peter Hill, an investigative journalist who has reported on many miscarriages of justice, and who founded the programme *Rough Justice*, in 1980, describes the main causes of poorly published accounts as being editorial problems of ignorance and commercial pressures.

In November 2002, miscarriage-of-justice-survivor Winston Silcott was granted his first escorted town visit, a measure taken by the prison authorities towards preparing lifers for eventual release after long-term imprisonment. From the moment he stepped outside the prison gates, Silcott was followed and photographed by two journalists for a three-page spread in the *Sun*.[7] They depicted Silcott as a

> ...grinning 6ft 6in giant murderer who mingled
> with unsuspecting families in a mall,

while making references to the horrific murder of PC Blakelock.

In 1987, Silcott and two other black men – Engin Raghip and Mark Braithwaite – were convicted of murdering PC Keith Blakelock during the riots on the Broadwater Farm estate in North London. On the second day of the trial,

The *Sun* published a photograph of Silcott and the accompanying caption read:

> This is the first picture of the man police believe wielded the machete that hacked brave bobby to death.[8]

Police at Paddington Green Police Station took the photo. Silcott had been woken from his cell then pinned against a wall by three officers. Believing he is about to be beaten, his face in the photo expresses a mixture of fear and bewilderment at being suddenly woken. Only the police could have passed the photo to *The Sun* with such inappropriate timing.

Bizarrely, it never seemed to have crossed the minds of journalists to take a close look into the case for themselves before printing the story. If they had they would have discovered that there was no evidence linking Silcott to the murder. Police took more than 1,000 photos of the Broadwater Farm riots and none of them showed Silcott to be present. There was no forensic evidence linking him to the murder but he was found guilty on the basis of a statement that he always denied making.

Indifferent to his plight, journalists allowed themselves to be fed snippets of malicious slander and once he was convicted, press coverage included:

> Victim of the Savages... Machete monster Silcott jailed for 30 years yesterday....
>
> > The *Sun*

The Face of Evil... This is the man with murder in his eyes and hate in his heart. Silcott led the baying mob which hacked PC Blakelock to death in the Broadwater Farm riots... The charge was like a scene from Zulu.

Today

In 1991, all three men had their convictions overturned when Electrostatic Document Analysis (ESDA) tests proved that police officers had fabricated Silcott's statement. Mark Braithwaite had been denied access to a lawyer. Silcott, however, had been convicted of another murder, that of gangster and amateur boxer Anthony Smith. He has always denied committing murder and insists he was forced to defend himself after being attacked at a party. Numerous witness statements, including those for the prosecution, support his claims and he expects to take his case to the European Court of Human Rights.

According to Silcott and all those who know him, he has been targeted and harassed by police officers all his life. It seems at least three other murders have been blamed on Silcott – but the police never had any proof to charge him with, other than evidence that they fabricated. In contrast, on the rundown estate where he lived, locals described him as a community spokesman who had always attempted to prevent conflicts. His family claim that racist police were determined to lock Silcott up and throw away the key. His mother, Mary Silcott, says,

From the age of fourteen the police started on Winston. Just riding a bike without lights, and they took him to court. From that day on they never stopped. They told me that if a pin dropped anywhere in Tottenham, they're coming for him and they're going to lock him away for life or send him to the madhouse.

Peter Hill explains that editors, like the police, can be pressured into 'slipshod methods' during murder investigations. In a racist society the problems are intensified.

People tend to watch and read what they wish to see. Public pressure fosters close, unhealthy relations between police and crime reporters. Each uses the other. The police feed reporters tantalising titbits that make sensational headlines. The headlines in turn help the police. The collusion continues when someone is charged and brought before the courts.

In Silcott's case the collusion seems to have continued for over a decade. The latest story, which appeared on 12 November 2002, was not motivated by truth, but by political bias. Readers were sinisterly warned that Silcott would soon be allowed out, 'WITHOUT a guard' if he behaved well. The paper went so far as to describe in boring detail what Silcott bought and ate during the whole visit, disappointingly adding (their italics),

He did not have to worry about the expense. It would barely have dented the £50,000 compensation he won from police.

In spite of being acquitted for Blakelock's murder, with his reputation further diminished through being sentenced for the murder of Anthony Smith, Silcott must now put up with being tracked by *Sun* journalists. They will link him to the murder of Blakelock for the rest of his life because for them his is a one-sided story. They have no wish ever to meet Silcott or hear from his family or the community he grew up in. Nor do they wish to view the case history or examine the evidence, though it is available. The role of these sorts of journalists is to frighten the public. If the public is scared into envisioning the release of some kind of dangerous, black devil, then the public will ultimately side with the police in their actions over the conviction of Silcott and their eternal wish to keep him locked up forever. They must not present an accurate, balanced story because then the public might have reason to think for themselves, which would be a terrible blow for those involved in locking Silcott away.

It is the truth that allows Silcott to keep challenging the system, no matter how long he is imprisoned or how negatively he is stereotyped in the process. To the community in Tottenham, black and white, he is a tower of inspiring strength. Many find it hard to believe that he survived his experiences and look forward to celebrating his return home.

For all the ignorance, there are also journalists who have succeeded in successfully uncovering injustices and exposing them in a political environment all too eager to cover up its failings. Don Hale dedicated eight years of his life to investigating the case of Stephen Downing.[9] Downing was seventeen and said to have had the reading age of an eleven-year-old when in 1973 he was arrested.

Downing had discovered Wendy Sewell lying in a Bakewell cemetery in Derbyshire, badly injured, and called for help. Police targeted him as their prime suspect and interrogated the vulnerable youth for eight hours without a solicitor present. They did not caution him but chose to pressure and bully Downing, shaking him violently, and yanking at his hair to keep him awake, until he confessed.

Downing always insisted that he had been told to sign a confession that he could not read and maintained his innocence for twenty-eight miserable years. If he had admitted his guilt he could have been released on parole ten years earlier. In 1994, Hale, the editor of a local newspaper, was approached by Downing's parents and asked to examine the evidence. When he realised how circumstantial the evidence was, Hale approached the police (rather naïvely perhaps but in good faith) in the hope that they could work together to challenge the conviction. By this time Stephen Downing had been in denial of murder for twenty-one years.

Right from the word go the attitude of the police was hostile and uncooperative. They insisted that all documents, forensics and exhibits had been burnt, lost or otherwise destroyed. It took Hale eight years to unearth all the material that he'd been told had been destroyed. As each piece of evidence came to light, he presented it to Derbyshire Police, C3 (the government's investigative unit before the CCRC came into being) and the Home Office. Hale was eventually able to prove beyond a shadow of doubt that the police evidence was flawed and that the police had flagrantly breached the Judges' Rules during Downing's arrest and interrogation.

By the time the case was finally referred to the CA

by the CCRC, it had emerged that the whole of the original crime scene had been cross-contaminated too. When Wendy Sewell was attacked, all the clothes at the scene were scattered around. The police photographed them, then picked them all up and threw them into a sack. Two days later Sewell died and the police returned to the scene to replace the clothes, shoes and murder weapon. For some reason Downing was charged with murder on the day of the attack, though Mrs Sewell did not die until two days later.

In January 2002 the CA overturned the conviction and Downing was set free. Both he and Don Hale appealed for the case to be reopened. Derbyshire Police agreed to start a new investigation, in spite of the fact that members of the force must have colluded to suppress evidence, and in that had actually succeeded for twenty-eight years.

To put it mildly, this was not the kind of behaviour that inspired trust or faith, but Bob Wood, Deputy Chief Constable of Derbyshire Police, tried to reassure a cynical public. He insisted that police procedures had improved considerably since 1973. Expressing regret that it had taken so long to quash the conviction he later stated that the target for an enquiry would be to ascertain whether there was enough evidence to arrest and charge someone else with the murder. In 1995, the same police force had threatened to jail Hale because he refused to disclose to them where and who his sources of information were. More than anything they had wanted him to drop the case.

Hale and the Downing family agreed to cooperate with the subsequent police enquiry but it was to end, unsurprisingly, in a complete fiasco.[10] The official report of the enquiry was released to the press during a stage-managed police press conference on 27 February 2003. Hale and members of the Downing family were deliberately excluded, so that they would have no opportunity to respond to the long list of allegations that would be suddenly sprung against them. David Sewell, the widower, was allowed to attend. A whispering campaign was about to swing into full force, with all the characteristic hallmarks of a police force desperate to win back some credibility.

At the press conference Hale was accused of withholding evidence, committing perjury and misleading the public in his book *Town Without Pity* (even though it had been produced three months *after* Downing's appeal). Following the standard pattern of what happens to victims of miscarriages of justice, and quite obviously determined to display every possible shred of incompetence, the police report went so far as to state,

> ...we have not been able to eliminate Stephen Downing from our enquiries.

Eager journalists lapped it all up, unaware that they were being used to play one of the oldest of police tricks. Unable to solve the crime, having made a total mess of the case from start to finish – and eventually being exposed as rather economical with the truth, to put it as mildly as possible – they may as well try and imply that they'd got the right person all along.

It had been a long, hard slog to get Downing's case back to the CA. For people who have been wrongly incarcerated it takes just as long and hard a slog to start rebuilding their lives. They have less chance of doing so if the police decide to start a new wave of abuse, aided and abetted by the media. As doubts begin to seep back into the community, there is one thing we can be sure of. No one who is guilty of causing and perpetuating the miscarriage of justice, *not one person*, will ever be held accountable. The effect is destabilising to say the least and as a result it becomes next to impossible for the victim of injustice to begin to move on.

There are óther journalists who have championed unpopular causes and even changed laws, sometimes at the expense of imprisonment for the deed. Despite the passing on of so much empty propaganda, the so-called dissent culture is alive and kicking, and I can count many such journalists working among the mainstream press. Out of a whole population, it is not possible to gag or train everybody to be passive forever. As people organise and try to change the political arena so too do journalists. There is by no means enough balanced coverage but what there is represents a significant effort to counteract the steady stream of depraved hysteria that spouts from some of our national newspapers.

In my most pessimistic moments I cannot help but worry though. Maybe Nick Cohen is right when, in his excellent book, *Cruel Britannia*, he writes,

> Resistance is tame because at the back of liberal journalists' minds is the nagging suspicion that the public do not want to be informed. (And in truth, it is difficult to sustain a belief in the intelligence of your fellow citizens when the *Sun* is the biggest-selling newspaper.)

It is easier to remain part of the uninformed masses and the saying 'ignorance is bliss' certainly rings true where justice issues are concerned, as I have discovered since embarking on this journey. I remain uncomforted, knowing certain 'things' about our system of justice in Britain. Maybe I should lull myself into a false sense of security and throw away all my research papers. I could pretend that all the prisoners illustrated in this book are a mere illusion and aim instead for consumer bliss.

On the other hand you never know when or why the finger of suspicion may one day point at you. It is as Cohen concludes.

> In the future, if you find yourself in trouble, do not expect the criminal justice system to help. Politicians and a senior judiciary composed of wealthy commercial lawyers with neither interest in nor understanding of human rights, will tell you that resources do not permit it.

And as your life is torn to pieces, if the crime you are convicted of is gross enough, you can be sure to find yourself slotted neatly in among the celebrity gossip, trivia and scandal, in the sensational crime section.

---

1 The Parole Board website can be found at www.paroleboard.gov.uk.
2 Statement made by Giles Philip Humphrey. Educated at Oxford University, in 1994 he was charged with the importation of cocaine and served four years. He served this sentence at HMP Wormwood Scrubs and HMP Swaleside.

3 The full parole report can be found at http://www.nao.gov.uk/ publications/nao_reports/9900456es.pdf.

4 Keirle, op cit.

5 *The Observer*, 20 January 2002.

6 Raymond, Joad, *Making the News, An Anthology of the Newsbooks of Revolutionary England 1641–1660* (Windrush Press, 1993).

7 *The Sun*, 12 November 2002.

8 Legal Action for Women, *A Chronology of Injustice: The Case for Winston Silcott's Conviction to be Overturned* (Crossroads Books, 1998).

9 Hale has written a book about his investigations into the Downing case called *Town Without Pity* (Century, 2002).

10 *New Statesman*, 10 March 2003.

5

PRISONERS INSIDE

Paul Blackburn

When I first met Paul he'd served twenty-five years as a discretionary lifer and had recently been granted town visits, having finally touched down at a Category D jail. I learnt that the Discretionary Lifer Panel (DLP) had been against the move to open conditions, but Helen Jones, his solicitor, had argued the case with expertise. An interview took place in the sunny gardens of a roadside café, somewhere between Boston and HMP North Sea Camp.

Always wary of meeting strangers, especially those who've spent time in the worst institutions of Britain, I observed Paul as discreetly as I could, feeling ridiculously nervous. I got the feeling he was far more wary than I, as well as weary of meeting strangers, and I secretly dreaded an awkward encounter. Learning of his town visits, my obvious preference had been to meet outside the prison if possible, yet in one of his letters he'd said that the second town visit he'd had turned into one of the worst days of his life. In his words,

> I just felt so alienated and exposed and so much pain that I couldn't enjoy it at all. It may sound daft but I wanted to run back to jail and hide. More than anything I just wanted to cry but I couldn't – I can't cry anymore.

As we began to talk, and I started to ask questions, I was to bear witness to a lone, seemingly gentle soul that was overflowing and overwhelmed with anguish, pain and blazing defiance.

September 2001, HMP Grendon

I was arrested on 21 July 1978 for the attempted murder and buggery of a nine-year-old boy. I had been interviewed several times as part of the investigation but only in the sense that they took statements from everybody living in the local area. I was fourteen years old at that time and normally resident at Red Bank Approved School in Newton-le-Willows where I was under a care order for offences of arson and theft. The arson was against my school.

I was on weekend home leave at the time of this offence, which was 25 June 1978. The only thing I knew about it was from when my sister's boyfriend and I had been out messing around on some waste ground near my house. We ran into lines of police and as we both had records we made ourselves scarce. When I mentioned this back at school, all they could say was that I was 'expressing an unnatural interest' in the offence.

The statements I gave to the police about my movements that weekend were quite brief and mostly inaccurate because

I didn't have a watch and times were expressed as 'dinner time' etc. In my first statement I think it mentions my having my hair cut but I don't ever remember saying this. Two women who worked on my unit at the school gave contradictory dates of when I did have my hair cut and I don't remember one way or the other, but claims were made that I had my hair cut to change my appearance.

The description of the person who committed this offence was given as having long, curly, ginger hair, being sixteen to eighteen years of age and five foot seven to five foot ten in height, with a Manchester accent. I'm not too sure about that as this particular description comes from a Home Office dossier so can't be trusted other than as a general guide. Anyway, I didn't fit the description at all but didn't mind giving statements to the police even though I was naturally wary and wouldn't go out of my way to speak to them.

I had a couple of previous convictions for theft and arson, arson being the most serious, but in general it was petty theft and vandalism. I didn't have much of a home life and avoided going home as much as possible. My whole family were terrified of my dad who used to beat us up. When we learnt that he'd drowned in 1978, my older brother Fred said, 'Thank God,' and it may sound bad, but we were all glad.

I was always out with mates, usually up to mischief I admit, but never alone. Also I had always admitted and pleaded guilty to anything I'd ever done – this was later in court made out to be that I was an 'experienced, street-wise criminal', even though I'd only ever been in juvenile magistrates' court twice.

Things took a very different turn on 14 July. I'd just come back from a camping trip and two police officers came to the school, took my clothes, and stopped me going on home leave. They questioned me more about Fred than myself really and kept on at me to tell them where he'd been on the day of the offence. Eventually I broke down in tears and told them he'd been working while still on the dole. They seemed to be satisfied with this and left though as it happens I was wrong anyway as he wasn't working that weekend at all. I didn't know at the time but these particular officers had already literally picked him off the streets and interrogated him all day and night. They later claimed to not know that he was in the police station until my brother Harry and then my mum turned up looking for him.

Fred had eventually made a verbal confession but retracted it. As far as I know he was never questioned about why he made this confession (I don't remember him being called as a witness either) or why he retracted it. He should have been asked because it would have shown a pattern of behaviour by the police who arrested me. Two other people also confessed to this offence but as far as I know, neither were taken seriously. These two police officers also told Fred that it didn't matter which one of us they got but they'd definitely get one of us.

I eventually got granted my weekend home leave so I learned all this when I got home. My mum told me she had been in touch with a solicitor about it and I should ask for them if the police ever came near me again. I had never used or seen a solicitor before and didn't even know that I could ask for one until I was told.

The same two police officers came to interview me again on 21 July 1978. I wrote another statement that took about an hour I think, so it was about ten o'clock in the morning. When I finished, they binned it and really started to give it large. I shit myself but I was a pretty fucked-up kid anyway and when they said they had statements from a previous offence and were going to charge me with three more attempted murders, I knew I was in big trouble.

The further charges related to a previous record of ABH with a co-accused Barry Hamilton. We were twelve years old and four other boys had been involved who were aged nine to ten. In mid-1976 Barry had made them strip off and bullied them by making them mess about with each other. The day before the police arrested me, they'd been back to interview the boys and got statements from them which suggested that there was a more sinister overtone to the offence and that it had been me who had been the prime mover.

It's only recently that one of the victims has actually endorsed my version of the real events in that case. It not only backs up what I say but I feel it also shows how the police were prepared to bend the evidence to suit themselves.

One important point in the statements mentions my using a knife – a blue-handled penknife. Well I didn't, although I did own one. They knew this, because when they forced a confession out of my brother Fred, they went to our house, searched his room and found my penknife. It was said that a 'white-handled' penknife was used in the 1978 offence. Later this was changed to 'a knife' so was dismissed by the judge as immaterial. Also, the knife had rust spots on the blade which they made out was blood. Fred must have told them it belonged to me so the police had it included in the statements. I didn't know at the time as they never showed me these statements.

The police suggested that the 1976 ABH was far more serious than first thought but it wasn't in the sense that we didn't admit it. At the time, the police put it down to a case of bullying and didn't charge us with indecency because of our age – twelve. No record of these facts has been found and I discovered that my approved-school file had been destroyed when I asked for it.

Anyway, back to what happened on 21 July 1978. The police threatened me with further charges and kept asking if I'd done the same thing to this nine-year-old boy as what Barry, my co-accused, had done in 1976. Then they began to get more specific, saying, 'You did this and then you did this and this.' They kept telling me that it was the same offence as the 1976 offence. Details were given to me about the offence so I knew where it had happened and I knew the area very well anyway.

I asked for my mum but was ignored. I asked several times and as many times for a solicitor but I was just blanked. One of the housemasters at the school was present but he just sat in a corner and never said a word. This went on for a couple of hours until I eventually started crying and looking to him for help. He basically just said, 'It's up,' and shook his head. This went on and on – I wasn't getting any help, so in the end I said I'd done it and would write a statement. They wouldn't let me just get up and walk out – they'd cautioned me and I thought that meant I'd been arrested so I couldn't go. They'd taken my shoes off me anyway. As I wrote the statement I had one of them standing over me, the bald one who had been aggressive before. He kept making suggestions and comments about what I said, like 'Are you sure it was that way and not this way?' and correcting me. I would have said anything to please them and I even wrote the statement myself as they went through the details with me.

I was taken to the police station where I asked to make a retracting statement but was ignored and then I was taken on to Risley. I had been at Risley for about five seconds and because I was still in shock and didn't answer to the reception screw when he asked me my name, he leaned over the desk and punched me in the face. I was hardly expecting it and fell over. I didn't see who it was but one of them grabbed me by my hair and half lifted, half dragged me out of the room, bouncing me off all and any obstructions along the way to one of the sweat boxes - my welcome to the big house. I basically got slapped, punched and kicked through the reception and over to the hospital. I was asked by a screw called Reese what I was in for and I said I hadn't done anything. I wonder if that ever got put into the daily occurrences book they have?

I found jail to be much like approved school and home - just something else to survive and my first line of defence was to withdraw into myself - nothing gets out and nothing gets in. From then on and a long, long time I was very, very isolated. I saw the shrink there, a Dr Lawson. He got a lot of criticism in the Judith Ward case and was pretty much discredited I think. I saw him first for about ten minutes where I denied everything but gave a brief account of the actual charge. When I next saw him he said I'd confessed to him and then got up and left after about two minutes. In his report for the court he says I confessed to him but he gives no details. He says it was almost word for word what I wrote in my statement to the police. Would he have ever had or seen that? But he also claims to have spoken to the police who arrested me. He discusses the existence of evil in his report - meaning me! Later psychiatric reports have condemned his report as biased and unprofessional.

I got a solicitor on Legal Aid who saw me once and interviewed me before my trial and that's it. I had no idea of what the hell was going on, I had no idea of their case against me and I never got any depositions until about fourteen years later. It was basically all done 'in my best interests' as I was a juvenile and I was never really included in anything. I remember going up for committal but I didn't have a clue what was going on or why - I didn't know what committal was.

Come my trial (Chester Crown Court) I had even less of a clue as to what was going on. I met the barrister and QC for the first time on the morning of the trial and supposed they knew everything about what was going on and what I wanted to say, etc.

I had two trials; the first was to determine admissibility of evidence, which was basically my statement which I said was not true. I don't remember too many details of the day-to-day running of the trial except that I was very frightened, didn't know what was going on and that I was extremely embarrassed about the sexual nature of the offence. Every time I spoke I was just accused of changing my story and told to conform to the paperwork. They only relented when I explained that I didn't have any paperwork.

I didn't eat or drink very much that week (don't know if that was recorded but I was told off about it by the screws) and was kept in extremely hot cells below the castle so I wasn't feeling very well at all. To determine accessibility of evidence the judge relied on the housemaster present at the interrogation who said that he didn't feel that any threats or coercion had been made.

There was a lot of interference by the judge. He constantly cut off my QC, answered for the police in the witness box and this went on throughout the trial. The police made some big screw-ups; they half admitted to giving me details of what they expected me to say and half admitted to threatening me. The two police didn't give the same story but my QC missed this until after the judge ruled that the evidence was admissible. He then said it could only be re-opened during the trial if full disclosure was made to the jury but my QC wouldn't do this as it would've meant telling the jury that I had a previous conviction (which, to the police, now appeared very similar to this one, with me having no way of disproving this lie).

The trial itself meant it was now up to me to prove that I couldn't have done it. I think my mum and brothers (Harry and

Fred) gave evidence to say that I was at home at the time of the offence. The prosecution story was that I had committed the offence after I had been out with my school friend Tony in the morning and early afternoon. They said that I saw some boys in the area along with the victim and went back on my own after leaving Tony at Harry's house. This was never established (nor was the time) but they said that when I left I didn't go home but headed in the opposite direction.

I still say that I went back to Harry's in the early afternoon then went home for something to eat. After, I went out to look for my friends who always used to hang around the shops. I hung around for a bit but nobody was about so I went back home. I played records and the radio for a while in my room then went downstairs to watch TV.

The prosecution said that I got back from Harry's much later and left in the opposite direction (going home I turn past the window of the house and going the other way I don't but nobody ever figured this out), going back to the waste ground and attacking the boy.

I cannot dispute the evidence of the crime itself but I do know that the boy wrote two statements – one before my arrest and one after. The one written after changes certain things like the hair colour is changed to be more like mine and 'white-handled penknife' is changed to just 'knife' (the police took a brown-handled Indian dagger off me). Other comments were added like 'I know boys of fifteen' (which was my age by then but I was fourteen at the time of the offence) 'who are as big as the one that attacked me.'

Other statements were taken after my arrest. The neighbour who found the boy claimed that he asked Leslie what had happened to him and his reply was that 'A big fourteen-year-old lad had bashed him up.' My age change was actually charted, but if the boy had said this then why wasn't it part of the description given before my arrest?

As nobody could say precisely what time I got home it was back to circumstantial evidence, saying that I could have done it. Again my QC tripped up the police and housemaster, and again got half admissions of threats and coercion but again they weren't followed up. In the judge's summing up he basically skimmed over the defence case. Seeing as he'd taken more part in the trial than everyone else put together nobody else got much of a word in. The jury did come back for instruction as they were confused over the contradictory statements but the judge told them to ignore it and only to accept evidence given in the box.

As far as I know the jury's decision was unanimous. The judge gave me life detention on the grounds that I needed to be contained until safe as per Section 53 (2) of the Children and Young Persons Act 1933. He said he didn't know how long it would be before I was 'safe' to be released but that he was sure I would not become lost in the system. I think that it is wrong to impose a 'life' sentence for these very reasons.

The judge did however order that a transcript of his and my QC's comments on sentencing should go with me as part of my prison file, as well as a copy of my statement to the police and the police notes. It was a discretionary life sentence although I didn't know this at the time.

I was kept in Risley for a while, firstly in the hospital dodging paedophiles (I was in a ward with adults), then I got sent to the young persons' wing. There, I was punched in the face until I wrote a request to go on Rule 43 for my own protection – not that I knew what that was. I can remember two old women (Board of Visitors) coming to my door and asking me why I was on Rule 43. I said I didn't know what Rule 43 meant and (in all innocence) said I'd only done it because a screw had hit me. So I got it again for grassing the screws up. I was kept in isolation for the next couple of months.

Some people came to see me from Glenthorpe, a juvenile detention centre. I don't know what they decided on but was later told that the Home Office had refused to send me there on the grounds of security. I also had two appeals but again, these were done 'in my best interests' and I knew nothing about them. It was obvious that I was one pretty fucked-up kid but nothing was ever done to help me.

My first allocation was to Swinfen Hall YP (young persons') Prison. I was the youngest person there and because of the nature of my conviction (which I always told everyone and said I was innocent) I was always fighting or getting beaten up. Just about everyday. It got worse and worse until one day I got hold of a dumbbell bar and went for the worst tormentors. I smashed their heads in with it, one at a time. There was no point going to the screws as half of them were worse than the cons and I was forever kicked, punched and slapped by them.

My first nicking was from a screw who just stood by when one guy threw hot water into my face while his mate laid into me. The screw ordered me to mop up the water and blood and I refused so I got nicked for refusing a direct order.

I wouldn't then and I won't now take any order from any screw. I wouldn't ever call them 'sir' and wouldn't accept anyone's authority. This meant I was viewed as subversive, disruptive, recalcitrant, unable to control myself or to be controlled, and as I wouldn't accept 'guilt' I was in 'denial'. I managed to survive by becoming a con. I was prepared to go the extra mile and fuck the consequences. I smoked lots of dope, knowing that I would never ever be released. For a long time I stopped speaking to people.

That's not the real me though. I'm easily found out by genuine people who see more of me than just all the front. I was tortured by years of abuse. I had all these people telling me how wrong and evil I was, that I didn't know my own mind – put together with everything else I was more fucked-up than ever.

Officially I was under the Joint Committee, a board of the Home Office and Parole Board. They did reports about me every two years I think but in them days it was all kept very secret and you were never told anything. I was moved to Blundeston, an adult Cat B in 1985 – that was pretty much a continuation of everything – forever in trouble, the only difference was discovering heroin. Heroin was beautiful – no pain! About the only positive thing I had in my life was that I had met Norma who was like the mum I'd never had. I had lots of fights still, got stabbed, did the same myself a couple of times, but I wouldn't shut up and I wouldn't back down – not then, not now, not ever. I didn't commit the offence and that's the truth. I had a Parole Board review there and they decided I should go to Grendon, a therapy unit. I only found out from my mate who was the hospital orderly and used to read my file for me. I applied for Grendon but was refused as I was still fighting my case.

I was sent to a Cat C at Acklington instead, in January 1988. Got into just as much trouble there. I used to play rugby and the PEI would give it large so I head-butted him. It was an unwritten rule that anything on the pitch stayed there so he couldn't nick me. Instead he got his gym orderlies to put the word out that I was a bad nonce [sex offender]. Loads more fights – got stabbed again when three guys in masks crashed into my cell but I still came out top. There was loads of trouble with the screws.

I had another Parole Board review, them now being on a twelvemonth basis. I had started going out as a community-service volunteer but was still refused an official escorted leave as I denied the offence. I got on well with the Number One Governor and Wing PO, who were a bit surprised to find out there was far more to me than reports liked to portray. They got someone from the Home Office down to see me. I guess they were case officers from the Lifer Management Unit [LMU]. They were surprised that I could converse intelligently as I guess the impression they had of me was the inarticulate kid who came into jail and learnt how to be a convict. I'd started to learn a lot more about what was going on, like what exactly a 'discretionary' lifer was and how the system could be challenged a different way from just spitting in anger at them.

I was in a Cat C (a very open one at that time) and things were beginning to look good. I used to sit and chat to the psychologist who said I didn't need any 'treatment', 'help', or whatever else they called it. One probation officer even sent my paperwork off to *Rough Justice* for me as she was so concerned. The expectation at the prison though was that I give up fighting for justice and just accept the status quo. I point-blank refused and all that I'd built up was eventually taken away from me. I got shipped out to Durham just a couple of months before my next Parole Board review. It meant my next review was a waste of time, as it was done by people I had never seen or spoken to before. My request to delay it was refused. I was sent on to another Cat C, Featherstone.

It was at Featherstone that I was to run into the new pet project, 'offending behaviour courses'. They didn't operate at Acklington or many other prisons by then, as far as I knew. My solicitors at the time (Birnberg) pressed for me to be reviewed under the new Discretionary Lifer Panels [DLP]. This involved a European Court ruling in 1990 that stated discretionary lifers were in effect sentenced under special circumstances and so should have their cases reviewed by a tribunal and not a politician. My DLP was Number 18, the eighteenth case held because it was argued that I should be dealt with as soon as possible.

I found out that I was something like four years over my tariff – by now it was a condition that you be told your tariff. Mine had been set at ten years! I think tariffs were only sorted out sometime in the early 1980s. I think it was set up by that slug David Mellor when he was in the Home Office. You were now told your tariff and the reasons and risk factors involved in 'your' offending act.

I'd got another board review in October 1992. I'd only been at Featherstone since February so there wasn't much people could say – I knew the gym staff from my youth-prison days but nobody else knew me that well. Still, I was recommended for open conditions and release as soon as possible by my wing SO, the chaplain (who I used to see every week) and the gym staff, but all these reports were suppressed. The reasons given were that they were 'repetitive and add nothing to what's been written already'.

The real reason is that only the view that I must 'address my offending behaviour by attending their courses' was allowed. I didn't know much about the board so I went along with things. No witnesses were called that I wanted. I wanted to challenge everything. The prevailing view was the prison psychologists who said I should attend a Sex Offenders Training Programme [SOTP] – I only saw them once and wanted to challenge them too. From a legal viewpoint, it was and still is the expectation that you go along with what's required of you. I told them that I can't then and can't now, as what's required is an admission of guilt as a starting point.

The board said that I should attend the course and gave me

another twelvemonth review, expecting me to have completed the programme by then, though there were only three Cat C jails that ran the course and only a few places available. The Home Office increased my review periods to two years, saying that I needed longer to do the course – what they really meant was that operational considerations meant that the course could not be done in twelve months. Basically, the fourteen years of jail time that I'd done up till then no longer meant anything and I was starting all over again, this time though with no prospects whatsoever of being able to get out.

I spent eleven months at Featherstone; for ten and a half months of that I was either pissed or stoned and a small group of us stuck together. I was included in the Liberty Campaign of 1992, in TV, national and local newspapers and radio. A list of over one hundred miscarriage of justice cases was published. I also got in touch with David Jessel's *Trial and Error* who started looking into my case. As I wasn't ever prepared to lay down and shut up, the lifer governor came to see me when I was in the block for not working (again!) and half an hour later I was put in a taxi. Supposedly I was going to Risley for visits but I ended up at Littlehey Hospital where I was told I was on hunger strike. It was a set-up, just to be rid of me. I did have a very erratic eating pattern anyway, often not eating for days or even weeks yet still training like a lunatic. I would drive myself into the ground then use drugs to keep me up. I suffered a great deal from depression and couldn't cope well when at my lowest.

I got moved from Acklington to Durham Hospital and back again, for psychiatric assessment and they used hospital procedure to move me to Littlehey then back to Featherstone. The screws kicked the shit out of me and I ended up in the hospital, not really the worse for wear – I always said screws fight like fairies! Losing all patience I flipped out for a while and to make it worse, someone really close to me died. I spent a month in hospital on very large doses of drugs. Free drugs, brilliant.

I was then moved to Usk having taken the advice of my home probation. It says in my DLP paperwork that this move was 'reallocation' – it was 'officially' for me to attend the SOTP but they can't say that as about six months later I was moved again for 'assessment' of the SOTP. Anyway, there never was an assessment – it was only ever a formality – by being convicted all prisoners required 'treatment'. Basically I was still expected to admit guilt as part and parcel of attending the SOTP. I had no intention of attending any so-called 'treatment'. Usk also turned out to be a VPU [Vulnerable Persons Unit] or Rule 43 by another name. I lasted a couple of months (three I think) before one of the cons gave it large and tried to bully me as he had his mate backing him up. I had to smack him and also chased his mate. All the rapists I was put amongst couldn't stand me because I wasn't like them. I was innocent and they hated me for it. I got done for assault (they claimed I'd hit him with a pool cue for no reason) but couldn't care less.

That same day I was moved to Cardiff down to the block where I stayed for about three months. The LMU tried to send me on to Dartmoor. I said that if they did, they'd better not take the cuffs off me. They tried to bribe me by saying that I would keep my Cat C. I asked to go to Wakefield instead because I knew it was a lifer centre and thought I'd get some sense there. Also my sister was coming over from the USA to visit me so Wakefield was ideal. I was sent there in September 1993. In transit at Leeds the screws from Wakefield refused to accept me as I was still a Cat C. I explained that I'd become a Cat B temporarily but it was a bad idea as, when I got there, I was stuck. Home Office policy meant that no lifer passes Cat B until they have 'addressed their offending behaviour'. Though there is a memo to all governors stating that claims of innocence should not prevent anyone making progress through the system, of course it does.

I had a bad time at Wakefield; got nothing but aggravation. I did their psychological assessments and they stated that I was sexually inexperienced! I've been locked up since I was fifteen, you don't need to pay some college twat £30,000 a year to work that one out! They demanded that I do an anger-control course and cognitive skills – I told them to fuck off. I then had another DLP and told them to fuck off as well.

I got sent to Gartree in 1994 where I met Gary Mills and Tony Poole who were also fighting their convictions. Good lads. They kept me on the straight and narrow and I started to get my head together a bit. The Home Office decided to move me to Full Sutton, a high-security jail. They said it was to take part in SOTP again; although the prisons ombudsman said that I should go back to Cat C the Home Office refused. Letters were exchanged between my MP Joan Lester and the Director General, Derek Lewis. Lewis claimed that I was sent to Full Sutton as it was close to where I lived and not because I needed secure conditions. Really, it was more punishment designed to bully me into cooperating with offending-behaviour treatment.

The only thing Full Sutton did for me was get me a bad habit going. I was on the lifer's wing with lots of lads who were doing thirty years so the message was that I was going nowhere. I had a great deal of support there from the lads but nothing could stop my downward spiral. I got stuck in the block and then shipped out to the Cat A unit at Durham in September 1996. I gave the screws the runaround and they sent me back to Full Sutton in November for my next DLP. My lawyers deferred the DLP as I still hadn't had an SOTP assessment. I got put in the block again after tearing up my cell, my head was in really bad shape.

I refused to leave the block for eighteen months and didn't really eat or look after myself for a while.

In January 1997 I was moved to Wormwood Scrubs after a riot at Full Sutton. There was a bit of a reception there, big steroid-head screws doing their chimp acts. I didn't speak to or acknowledge any of the screws, I didn't eat and slept on the floor beside the bed. I received lots of free drugs again! I did engage with David Thornton who was head of the Offending Behaviour Programmes at the LMU. It was Ruth Mann of his unit who had been blocking me for years. Thornton recommended that I be moved to Grendon but Grendon refused to accept me again as I was still challenging my conviction.

All the Wormwood Scrubs' screws working on the block ended up being suspended for brutality. Basically if you were black, Irish or mentally ill they used to give you a good kicking because that's what they used to enjoy doing. They wanted to move me out of there quickly before the enquiry team came in but were too late as I'd already named the worst of the screws to the guy who brought the case against them. The screws never even touched me or came close to it! Instead they gave me a TV and radio and left me out on the yard all day. They never managed to reach me. I was made to write to the Home Office promising not to assault anyone before they'd let me go to Brixton to do an enhanced thinking skills course. It was a load of shite but I did the course. This was now April 1998.

After doing cognitive therapy with a psychologist from Maudsley Hospital I got moved to Albany where they tried to engage me in 'being a prisoner'. I kept my nose clean trying to get moved to Grendon and finally got moved here in April 1999.

This is a strange place, Grendon. They do group therapy. I've dealt with a lot of things in my fucked-up life here but just as much remains. I'm still totally anti-authority; I'm still full of anger at the system and still prepared to go back to square one to fight nose-to-nose with the system, for justice for myself and anyone else.

This place is different though. You're given some trust I suppose. I've not touched drugs for years, I've re-socialised myself here as they hold conferences and debates with visitors and have family and lifer days. I had my next DLP in February. The usual views pervaded, i.e. I should do SOTP; others said that as I'm a Cat B I should move on to a Cat C. I told them all to fuck off. Release me or leave me alone. The governor went on the panel and said that I should go to open jail before release and the wing therapist agrees. My own doctor says I should be released into the hands of a care team. The board refused to release me but said that I should go to open jail in July.

I'm here, still waiting for the Home Office to finish reviewing my move to open conditions. At the moment I'm pretty messed up again. Depression and too long in jail. But nothing untoward and nothing that will ever be put right. The saga continues and it's now September 2001…

JANUARY 2002, HMP GRENDON

I may make it to the London New Bridge Youth Conference this year at long last – I've been invited to the last two and not been able to go and speak at them. The London regional co-ordinator, a good friend of mine, wants me to speak at their conference – I'll shit myself but it'll be good experience! We have conferences here every three to four months, usually on a theme but as much a Grendon 'selling exercise'. Still, they're good for me, socialising, as they have sixty to seventy visitors from all over the place and all fields. I had to speak at one of them from the stage – I'll fight anyone if I have to but fuck speaking publicly – that's scary!

That's been about it for this place for me, re-socialising, conferences, family days where family and friends come on-wing for the day and we have dinner etc. Then there are social evenings, which are for 'professionals' such as your probation officers. We also do debates with the University of Central England as their professor is David Wilson. He used to work for the prison service but resigned in protest at conditions, brutality etc. I was principal speaker at the last one, debating criminality: *Nature or Nurture*. I was with one guy who wanted to be a copper and a lass who wanted to be a prison governor! (The youth of today eh? So unsociable!) Anyway, I had them over good style. Mind you it helped to quote from David Wilson's books as he chairs the debate!

As for the rest of this place? It's a nuthouse and drives me fucking mad. Therapy is bollocks. Well, for me it is as the only thing I've found out is that actually I'm normal. Well, as normal as I can be under the circumstances. I've also found out there's nothing in this or any jail that can help me. They're the problem not the cure. They can try all they like but they can't take the truth from me.

Still, I've met some good, honest people here, individuals that is, not the system as a whole, because it denies me who I am and wants me to be who they think I should be based on some fucked-up court case. Fuck them, I've fought twenty-five years for my identity and integrity and I am not giving it up for nothing or nobody.

Actually, I saw Val the doc the other day. She keeps me on a low dose of anti-depressants now and then. She said she'd rather have me on 225 ml (which would kill an elephant I think) as she says, 'Prison is the problem and you need psychiatric care on release' – not like the doctors I used to know. I used to see them appear at the cell door in the block behind two massive, hairy-arsed screws. 'Fit? Yes, right,' and they'd be gone, leaving me standing there bollock-naked with fat lips, black eyes and lumps on my head.

Anyway, hopefully I'll be away and out of this place soon. The psychologist did what they call a static risk assessment, which means that as I deny guilt and refuse to 'address my offending behaviour' I represent a high risk of offending. The Parole Board binned this report though as it's neither based on anyone or anything specific. It's just a formula the Home Office hand out to use. It's that that has kept me in for another ten years to date, and is why they chucked me into dispersals as a punishment because I wouldn't bow down. They made a mistake sending me to Full Sutton though, which was full of good people (cons that is) and they got me through.

What else? There was a hundred and one things I meant to mention but my head's a bit tired. I've been very restless and distracted for a while and it makes it difficult to sort things out amongst all the thoughts constantly racing through my head – it never ever stops and it burns me out. I can't touch the wacky baccy to slow things down. I haven't touched anything for five, six years now as it got too heavy. I wanted to blot everything out and ended up doing more harm than good. It ended up that the drugs just didn't work anymore which was a bit of a bugger.

My MP Ian Stewart has taken on a bit of a role in chasing the Home Office about getting me moved on. He sorted a meeting out with Boateng who then changed job. It left it open for the LMU to have me over again and start playing up so instead of me going to Cat D in June/July, they decided to review me again. Anyway, eight and a half months later I've now got Cat D but they still won't offer me a day out here. I've actually had to apply for one – not that they've ever given me anything here in nearly three years! I must not be of the right mind. Next they'll want me to explain why I would want a day out. It's all a game I know but I've always said fuck their game, I ain't playing.

I guess it's why I've had problems with this Cat D business. I feel like Judas. Why the fuck should I ask these people for anything, it's them who should be asking me to forgive them. They're the criminals not me, as I certainly don't go locking people up for fuck all. I sit on these endless bloody review boards and it makes me want to rage. I want to hate the people on them, and everyone around me, but I can't. It's not me and I can't hate anyone. I've seen enough pain for three lifetimes' worth and I can't do it to anyone else. Sometimes I feel like a coward for it though. I think of friends – innocent people – who are still on the front line and part of me wants to be back there with them. At least I knew where I stood then.

April 2002, HMP North Sea Camp

Things have been moving on a bit for me here, good and bad. I'm on my first escorted day out on the 16 April (I have to do two escorted before I get them on my own at the beginning of June). In general I'm getting on okay and this place is a piece of piss really. All the bollocks about Cat Ds is just that! Not that anyone is taking any notice (officials that is). They have their programme and you will follow it come what may, whether it's appropriate to you or not. And it's not, but there you go.

I've been on to my MP Ian Stewart and the LMU to see if they will hurry things up. I should have been in Cat D by July last year, so by rights I should have been on my home leave by now. I had to have a sit-down meeting with the lifer governor and there is no way of communicating with him, he's a spiteful bully. He's got a big problem with me fighting my case and is forever having digs with me about it. I've been in an absolute rage and had to really control myself, as the reality is that I want to punch him in the face and treat him like the bully he is. I can't though can I? I wish such feelings would go away, but they don't do they? Everyone thinks that everything should be okay now that I'm here.

I'll stick with it though and do what I can. I still get too many days when I can't see anything in front of me. I'm still stuck in the middle of everything because I've been locked up since I was fifteen and want to live my life so much. I've wasted in these places yet can't walk away from the fight even if I wanted to. It's justice and truth and a part of me I can't change, but I regret it because it wasn't my burden to carry and should never have been loaded on me, and I just have to try and deal with that.

Do these feelings ever go away? Will the rest of my life be infected with such pain? Will I pass it on to those I love? I suppose it's passed on already. I'm hurt and so badly damaged by the years in these places but I don't want to spend the rest of my life reliving it. I want to get married, have kids, have a good steady life, not too much to ask for is it? These people here reckon they're 'helping' me and won't accept that what's been done to me is torture. There's no point me even saying it now as every time I open my mouth, I'm told that I'm taking backward steps and they threaten to punish me for it. I feel like letting them get on with carrying out their threats.

I was sent to see the careers service too. The board actually decided that I should do a forklift drivers' course. I wondered if they were going to hand me a shovel too, the patronising bastards. (Still, three days out of here to do it would be okay by me.) I want to go to college to study journalism. I'm also looking at the Open University at the moment for sociology as it involves media, youth offending and criminology in some modules.

AUGUST 2002, HMP NORTH SEA CAMP

I struggle to read at the moment as I feel so distracted, uncomfortable and unable to relax. I love books though. At the moment I'm reading *Snow Falling on Cedars* by David Gutterson - trying to read I should say - a few pages at a time. I sleep about two hours a night. Being here, we get our own rooms and can lock the door and all that. A novelty in itself but if anyone walks within ten feet of the door I wake. It's not like I'm leaving the door wide open and I've got like fifty cons and screws walking around me. But I still wake. My mind'll suddenly be going at a 100 miles an hour in the middle of the night.

People say I'm almost out and yeah I guess, physically I almost am. I've got my body out of jail but that's about it. I've not got the rest of me out of jail. I'm having a rough time with a lot of things. Can't seem to get any answer at all about anything here. I sorted a job for myself and then was prevented from doing it. I'm working at a residential and day care centre for mentally handicapped adults - it's a great job and so rewarding but I really need a properly paid job. It's all about taking steps and I wish the screws wouldn't actively hinder me. I got paid £2.49 this week, that's for a full week's work and nobody seems to see that there's a problem! I can't sleep and I'm weary to the bone. The usual camp screws' retort to me is, 'You'll find yourself back in a Cat B.' Excuse me while I wet myself I'm so scared. I will not put a foot wrong as much as they'd love me to.

I do love being out and having new experiences now although the first few times were terrible. Paddy's plans sound like a fantastic idea. I can picture it already and also ache for the isolation of fields and space. To be far from the scurrying madness of life here is something I've dreamed of. I know I need time and space to repair myself but I'm just not getting it. The hostel I'm being forced to stay in for my 'home leaves' could go by the name of any other institution I've already been in. It's no different. Home isn't home and I wonder where I really belong. I did go home but it was just too weird for words. I didn't feel comfortable or welcomed and it was as if I was an extra in a play – there but not included.

In 1994 Bob Duffield, working for *Trial and Error* (before their budget was cut by Channel 4), met Paul and began an investigation into his case, because he felt haunted by the fear that Paul was innocent. During Paul's five-hour interrogation, he hadn't been allowed a solicitor or his mother present. The senior housemaster offered Paul no protection whatsoever and having studied Paul's confession, Duffield concluded that it was unlikely that such an ill-educated, troubled child could have written with such precision and vocabulary. In addition, Paul did not match the description of the attacker. It was a hideous crime, committed in broad daylight and the police apparently took more than 2,000 statements. Duffield could not find any of these statements but knew that three other youths had confessed. Through his research, Duffield discovered that Paul was the wrong age, wore the wrong clothes, had different coloured hair (his is blond) and the knife he owned was completely different from that described by the victim, when he was arrested.

The worst thing about this case is that all the forensic exhibits disappeared from the forensic science laboratories before the trial. They could have proved his innocence.

The CCRC have now been investigating Paul's case

for about five years. David Jessel joined the CCRC as one of their commissioners but sadly, cannot have anything more to do with the case. During my interview with David Britten, acting Head of Information for the CCRC, he stated, 'David Jessel does totally exclude himself from anyone he's had an involvement with through his TV programme. If he didn't, people would say he had a bias.'

This surprised me and I replied, 'But surely he would be justified? I mean he hasn't involved himself with miscarriages of justice on a whim. Surely his experience and the knowledge he gained brought him here in the first place.'

Britten shook his head. 'We are a reviewing organisation. It depends what the remit is and ours must be one of impartiality.'

David Jessel and Bob Duffield investigate Paul's case and find out that he was the wrong description and age; there are allegedly 2,000 witness statements now missing; two police officers involved allegedly altered a previous conviction and made it into something it wasn't; there were three other confessions; the psychiatrist involved was the same one who had been criticised for non-disclosure of evidence in the Judith Ward case – all this collective evidence and he'd served almost twenty-six years to boot, denying guilt all the way. Then David Jessel becomes a commissioner at the CCRC and nothing can be done for him.

Sue Lucas-MacMillan

Locked up alone, your thoughts often wander to memories of the loved ones you have beyond the bars that cage you. You wonder what they look like, wonder about their daily habits, their lives, their loves and their passions. Stuck in stasis in that cell, time deceives you and you can only remember what they were like before you went away. Your memories are locked in a fixed image while time and people move on around you, never standing still like you are.

To be upped and ripped away from your loved ones is the hardest thing any of us could possibly deal with. To have them suddenly disappear from your life, except in memory, is one of the worst punishments the system can put you through. But what if the reasons the system used to lock you up were founded on lies, mistakes and incomplete and inconsistent investigations? I remember the last time I was with my two sons, Conor and Christy. Riding in a taxi one night having just kissed them goodnight, I was arrested for murder. So, in 1995 my babies were taken away from me and forced into foster care while I was in remand. Two babies of six months old and eighteen months old forced to be separated from their mother. Christy was still being breast-fed at the time. Conor was in the process of learning to walk and talk. Both were still heavily dependent on their parents. However, with a drug-using father and a mother in prison, they only had each other to lean on.

As well as taking the support of their mother away from these boys, they have been informed repeatedly by Social Services (their 'carers') that their mother is a murderer. Let down by the state and the Civil Service, they have been separated and moved from foster home to foster home, away from each other and from their mother. These 'carers' are supposed to form a support structure for those in their care, shielding them from any news, events or behaviour that might have an adverse effect on their development and growing up. However, the story of these two boys only demonstrates how each year, thousands of children are failed by those who hold direct care and parental responsibility for them. With their entire parental structure taken away, they only have each other for love, comfort and support. And so they are kept apart, firmly entrenched in a vicious circle perpetuated by the state. Divide and conquer tactics worked for the British Empire, now it's happening in our own streets and homes.

Once a week, I'm allowed to talk to my kids. Each week I assure them that I am okay. The only thing that keeps me going, that gets me out of bed in the mornings, is the knowledge that Conor, my eldest son, understands and knows that I am innocent and that I do not belong behind bars. This is what empowers my fight.

On Saturday 11 March 1995, I was accused of killing an elderly woman, Muriel Hadfield. I was in a taxi, on my way to buy some heroin from a pub in Hulme. I only expected to be gone for a short while but on the way to the pub, Greater Manchester Police stopped my taxi and I was arrested. I was taken to Platt Lane Police Station where I was informed of Ms Hadfield's death. It was the first I had heard of it.

I grew up in a large family of over ten siblings in council housing in Manchester. A poor upbringing led to degrees of truancy and petty theft, which resulted in me ending up in an approved school. On leaving, I won a scholarship to do a course where I would learn how to be a keypunch operator. I spent three days there before leaving. The next few years saw me fall into trouble with the law for various offences and I spent a six-month sentence in jail when I was just twenty. I drifted through my twenties with no direction and little self-esteem, working as a prostitute, and as a dancer in Amsterdam.

On 26 January 1991, my life changed forever. A taxi driver forced me to a secluded location, beating me till I lost consciousness and raped me. I fell into a really bad state following this and found it hard to deal with. I still do but at the time I was beside myself with anguish and found it so hard to keep living. I turned to heroin and cocaine to try and block out the pain and trauma.

While using drugs, I met and had a whirlwind romance with Dougie, who I married two months later. Conor was born in 1993 and for the duration of the pregnancy I managed to stop the drugs. It was important to me to have my child be born clean. The following year, I was only an occasional user and my second son Christy was born, again drug-free and healthy. By this time Dougie was on a methadone programme.

Following Christy's birth, I suffered from a severe case of post-natal depression. I turned to heroin again to help get me through mundane daily household tasks. I was depressed and would cry for no reason. There were occasions when I couldn't face doing the children's washing and would just buy them clean clothes from my benefits and social security money. Between Dougie and me, we started doing around three bags of heroin a day. I funded both of our habits by pretending to be a prostitute, only this time I was determined never to have sex with any of them. I had this scam where I would lure punters in and get them to pay up front. I would then tell them to wait while I cleared out a room for them and then disappear down the back alleyways that I knew so well. I managed to do well enough. Dougie would collect bric-a-brac from skips and sell them on to second-hand shops and scrap merchants. He would always bring home bits of material for me as I had a fondness for sewing.

At this point, we received £120 a week social security money as well as £18 child benefits. This was not enough for our family of four. Hooked on the drugs again I began to feel more desperate the broker we got, and so a few weeks before my arrest, I took to walking around the area we lived in, begging for money, using excuses like needing the money for bus fares.

The day of my arrest, Dougie had managed to sell some things from skips to a shop. With the money he received, he bought us a bottle of vodka. I finished half of the bottle within an hour, mixing it with cream soda. Because I had mixed it, I was not as drunk as I otherwise would have been. Between 7.30 p.m. and 8 p.m. I walked through the alleys to make some money from 'prostitution'. I had two punters, and between them earned £75. I instructed them to follow me to my house but I easily lost them. Dougie called a taxi for me and I was driven to the Claremont pub on Claremont Road, where there was usually someone standing out front selling heroin. This time there wasn't so I got the taxi driver to take me further along to another dealer on Broadfield Road. Here, I purchased a £10 bag of heroin and was dropped off back home. Dougie and I smoked the entire bag between us, and decided that I should go and buy some more. He called a taxi for me from the same company I had used earlier.

I kissed Christy and Conor goodnight as I did every night without fail and promised them to be home soon. I was wearing the same clothes I had been wearing all day: a light-green jumper, black cords, brown shoes and a long navy overcoat. I was wearing these same clothes when I was arrested. My long, dark, curly, frizzy hair was tied back into a ponytail, disguising its bushiness. The taxi arrived and I left to go get the drugs. I never returned home because I was arrested on suspicion of killing Muriel Hadfield.

According to a description, the perpetrator fleeing Hadfield's flat was a woman aged thirty to forty, who was half-caste with fuzzy hair and who was wearing a green or a blue jumper, black ski-type pants and low-heeled shoes with no belts or buckles. My 'fuzzy' hair was tied back in a headscarf so there was no way that it could have been seen. The description was quite nondescript and could have been anyone. But the fact is I was known to the police for prostitution and loitering. This made me an easy target, someone to look convincingly grimy enough in the dock for a quick conviction. I am from society's underbelly so I suppose I'll do. Other contradictions with the description are that I've been told countless times that simply by looking at me, you cannot tell that I am mixed race or 'half-caste'. On the face of it I look more white than anything else – and I am – it was my mother who was half black. When I was arrested I was still in the same clothes that I had been wearing all day and my hair was still tied back with a scarf.

At the police station a doctor saw me because I was suffering from heroin withdrawal. The doctor said that I was fit for interviewing. I was ordered to provide intimate body samples without any consultation with a lawyer. I took the decision that I was happy to do so as I had nothing to hide. Various hair, nail and swab samples were taken. There was a full body examination that revealed a fingernail scratch on my neck, which they found questionable, obviously not taking into account the presence of very young children in my household. They had difficulty taking any blood samples from me because of my heroin abuse. When the doctor stuck the back of my hand with his needle, he managed to spill a lot of my blood onto the table and onto my hands and fingers. Worried that this would lead to mistakes or misunderstandings later on down the line, I made a point of pointing to the blood, saying that I wanted everyone to know that it was my blood.

Before the exam, the police had removed all my jewellery,

including a number of my rings. However my engagement ring would not come off my finger. The detective insisted that the ring had to come off. The doctor tried by pulling at it roughly until my finger started to go purple. The detective then threatened to cut the ring off but I objected, protecting what little I had left of my family in that room. Finally a swab was taken from under the ring.

I was intimidated by their constant questioning. They asked me when I had last been to Holford Avenue (the road that Muriel Hadfield lived on). I said that I had last been there one week ago as I sometimes asked people near my area for change, either on the street or by knocking on their doors, during the daytime. I would never steal, only ask, saying that I needed the money for bus fare or to help my diabetic mother. The policeman tried to force me to admit that I preyed on elderly people but that just wasn't true. A week before, I had stood on Muriel Hadfield's porch and asked her for money. Hadfield had given me a pound but I had not gone into the flat and I had never seen her again. I had not been near that block of flats since, especially not on the night of 11 March and as a result they could not find my fingerprints inside the flat.

When the interview ended I was put into a cell. My solicitor spoke to the officers and asked them why they had not put any evidence to me, but had merely asked for my movements. One of the officers got particularly upset about this and my solicitor remarked that this was my opportunity to comment on their version of events but I was not given the chance to do so. It was like the officers had already made their minds up about my guilt and merely gave me a chance to tell them what I had done instead of reacting to what they intended to pin on me.

The second interview was a lot more intrusive. The police told me that they had found a large amount of my hair in a bin in my house. I explained that sometimes I wore a hairpiece and that left hair on it. So the hair in the bin was probably from my hairpiece. At that stage they did not mention that any blood had been found on the hairpiece. They also showed me a small piece of material that had been found on top of my kitchen cupboard. They claimed it matched with material that the knife, found in the old lady's house, was wrapped in. This was the first time they had mentioned any of this to me but I do not recollect them mentioning that the knife was the same as one from my block of knives, which was missing. I was told that there was a whole team of scientists and forensic men at my house but I remained adamant that it was not my hair that would be found in the old lady's hand and there would not be any of my fingerprints in the house. At this point the police told me that hair strands found in the woman's hand matched my real hair. They even asked me if it was common for heroin addicts' hairs to fall out.

The police then claimed to have found bloodstains on the door in my bedroom. But as I explained, Conor had trapped his finger in our door and taken the top of it off. I told the police that it would be his blood that they had found on the door. Similarly with another bloodstained towel I was asked about, I explained that a few days previously Conor had fallen out of his pram and his lip had been bleeding. Why didn't they just test the blood? Living in a house with a baby and a toddler, one will be privy to cuts and scrapes and accidents. Yet here I was, sat and trapped, unsure of where the policemen were trying to lead me.

I was adamant throughout both interviews that the police could have any samples that they liked, that I would go on an identification parade, but that none of my fingerprints, blood or hair would be found in that old lady's flat because I was not responsible for her murder.

Little did I know that my innocence would simply not matter.

Less than a year later, on 5 March 1996, I was convicted of Muriel Hadfield's murder. The trial itself was less than extensive and lasted no more than seven days. The prosecution presented a short, flimsy list of accusations as proof against me. The main argument was that I lived 200 yards away from the murder scene and ten days before the murder I had been seen begging near Hadfield's house.

A witness who lived above Hadfield had heard a thud, gone downstairs to investigate and seen a woman coming from the direction of her flat. He described the woman as 'half-caste' with frizzy hair, in her thirties, medium build and five feet seven or eight. Another witness visiting someone in the same block of flats saw a mixed-race woman at 10.15 p.m., acting oddly at the end of the alleyway. He identified me at an identity parade but stressed he wasn't one hundred per cent sure I was the woman he had seen, while the first witness failed to identify me at all. These comments were excluded from the trial by the judge.

Another witness saw me at 10.10 p.m., running up the avenue where we both lived towards her, and twenty minutes later noticed a smell of burning coming from my garden. A piece of cloth matching another piece of cloth found at Hadfield's house was found at my house. The knife found in Hadfield's flat *could* have been the murder weapon (surely they would know for sure?) and a box set of kitchen knives at my house had two knives missing. A prosecution forensic witness claimed that there was 'strong support' for the knife that killed Hadfield originating from my box set. I tried to explain that I hadn't been the only person who had bought that same box of knives. A man called at a number of homes in the vicinity of my house, selling these blocks of knives for £2 each. Many of my neighbours had bought the same block as me and many had knives missing here and there. He wasn't the most scrupulous of characters. The cloth that the knife was wrapped in did match a piece of cloth in my house and the only explanation I can think of is that Dougie, my husband, would often bring scraps from the skips home and would include bits of cloth for me because I enjoyed sewing.

A hairpiece found at my house was bloodstained, analysis claiming it to be the same blood as Hadfield's. On the knife was a single hair, which was indistinguishable from a hair found at my house. There was also a single hair found on the coat that I was wearing that night. Neither strands showed any traces of blood on them.

This was the prosecution's evidence and though far from extensive was not properly rebutted in court by my lawyers. However, lurking doubts as to the conviction led to the following rebuttals of the medical and forensic evidence.

I was told that the bloody murder resulted in Hadfield getting blood on her hands and the front of her clothing, meaning the attacker would have evidence of blood on his or her hands as well. Blood was splattered on the wall next to the deceased and in and around other areas of the flat. The violence of the murder meant a struggle at close quarters. There were long, wavy hair strands on the door handle of the living room. However there was no DNA evidence to indicate a direct link between the murder scene and myself. Also, due to the amount of blood, whoever attacked Hadfield would have had blood-staining on their clothing as well. Yet, the only blood on my body that night was that resulting from the botched blood samples taken at the police station.

There was no sign of forced entry on Hadfield's door, even though ten days previously she had been wary enough of me to place a written description of me in a drawer near her door and phone the police about my begging. It is improbable that late in the evening she would have been willing to open the door to me again. There is also the issue of the timeline. The first witness heard the thud in her flat at 10.05 p.m. (the time was verified by what was being shown on the BBC at the time) and went to investigate.

The second witness saw a figure running away at 10.10 p.m. This leaves five minutes for someone to struggle with and kill Hadfield, leave the apartment and run back to the house. These two times do not correlate at all. The exact time that the first witness, Anthony Hopwood, heard the thud was confirmed by the television schedule and what he was watching. Half an hour later, I was seen by a student paramedic knocking on a neighbour's door. Then I was collected by a taxi. There is a very narrow timeline, only allowing me a mere thirty minutes to return home after a vicious bloody murder, dispose of any bloodstained clothes I would have been wearing and ensure there were no traces of blood on me. One has to bear in mind firstly that it was verified that I was wearing the same clothes all day and secondly that I had a lot of drink and drugs in my system. Thirty minutes would be a stretch for a sober person, but how the hell can anyone make incriminating bloodstain evidence (that would have been present on my clothes, if I had committed this gruesome crime) just disappear? And without me even changing my clothes?

It is a sad but true fact that my house was filthy as I was unable to clean it properly during my period of depression. The bathroom was recorded by the police as being filthy with a bath full of stagnant water, which had been there for some time. Within the bath was bedding, which had been there for a while as well. If I had returned covered in blood, which due to the bloody violence of the murder would have been a definite, I would have needed to wash somewhere. There was no way I could have washed in that bathtub and there were no splashes of blood around the bathroom or kitchen sink. In the timescale I was given I would have had to wash quickly, meaning a likelihood of being sloppy and leaving traces of blood on the surfaces. These were not found. There was no evidence of blood on any part of my body.

The crown's expert, Caroline Eames said, 'I have found no blood-staining on items of clothing or footwear relating to Susan MacMillan which could have come from Mrs Hadfield. Given the expectation that Mrs Hadfield's assailant would have been bloodstained, I consider the following to be the only reasonable alternative explanations for this finding: a) Susan MacMillan was not involved in this incident; b) she was involved but the submitted clothing was not worn at the time of the incident.' However, due to time constraints, as previously discussed, there was never time to change or to wash myself clean.

The witnesses were also flimsy. Hopwood described the woman he saw as 'half-caste with black hair, which was clearly frizzy and bushy'. However as previously stated it is hard to look at me, even in the clear light of day and describe me as mixed race. Also, my hair was tied up, meaning it was not clear whether it was frizzy or not. The second witness, Mr Tait, offered a description of the woman that did not match mine at all. He even put me in at five whole inches shorter than I am, which is a distinguishable amount. He also said that I was swaying back and forth as if I were on drugs. Not the actions of someone on a short timescale having just committed murder. One would assume a sense of urgency. He also said he saw someone with 'rotting or missing' teeth. At the time of the incident, I can assure you I had good teeth, which could not on any account be described as rotting. Despite what time has done to them now, they were not rotting back then. The woman he described was also going in the opposite direction to the woman seen by Hopwood. Mrs McIntyre, the neighbour who saw me running back to my house at 10.10 p.m., was not challenged as this was probably when I was running home having just conned my last punter out of money. The burning smoke McIntyre saw emanating from near the kitchen door of my house was not sourced and the debris, having been forensically identified, offered no proof that clothing or any other incriminating item had been destroyed in it. In fact, later McIntyre noted that the burning item looked like a piece of tinfoil. This is correct because the tinfoil under my cooker would often catch fire and I would have to throw it away. One of the officers on the scene did find a burnt piece of tinfoil in the bin.

The hairpiece that was found in my house that contained the blood of Hadfield was a complete mystery to me as I had not worn that particular one on the night and I honestly could not explain the presence of the blood. It was forensically identified as Hadfield's blood. The only likely explanation that I can think of is that it was planted there to help with an easy conviction of a junkie prostitute beyond any reason of doubt. It could have been taken from my house at the preliminary search and then covered in blood and replaced, as it was not immediately found. It was found a few days after I had been arrested. I wasn't even sure whether the damned thing was mine or not. It was a common hairpiece though and could be easily purchased in shops for £2.99. However, the oddness of this entire piece of evidence lay in the fact that if I had been wearing the hairpiece at the time of the attack, and it had become covered with Hadfield's blood, surely my own hair would contain bits of Hadfield's blood too? And there was no trace of any blood of any sort in my hair. As already discussed, the timeline would not have given me enough of a chance to wash my hair clean. And believe me, with my hair it takes a while. Therefore, for the blood to just congeal on the hairpiece only and not my hair is either a chance mystery or, in all likelihood, a fictional and flawed piece of evidence.

Rebutting the three main prosecution points, the witnesses, the knife, the bloody hairpiece, the lack of other significant forensic evidence that would be expected in other trials, make this one look flimsy. This raises a lot of doubt as to the validity of the conviction. You can't simply say that all the clothes were burnt and all traces of forensic evidence were destroyed, as it seems clear that time is an important factor in this case and I could not have reasonably achieved all that they claimed I had within the time constraints that existed.

On top of it all was the complete lack of a motive. I had hardly even met the woman, let alone have a reason to brutally murder her. What had she ever done to me? There had been a struggle and the flat was left in a mess; I was informed that there was jewellery lying near the deceased that had not been taken and other items in view that had not been touched as well as the lack of forced entry. This only points to the fact that perhaps the victim knew her attacker and there was a motive, as simple theft did not seem the reason. Hadfield's daughter described her mother as being security conscious. She had locks on all windows and locked all doors. She had a chain fitted on the front door, which she had a habit of using as well as a spy hole. If she had been so disturbed by me the first time she met me that she phoned the police, it is doubtful that with the ability to see who it was, she would have let me through the door.

Despite all this evidence to support my innocence, I was still convicted. A legal farce of a case. An elderly woman. A gruesome murder. A quick resolution. A junkie prostitute, caught up in a system where cruel words like 'She's probably done something wrong anyway so it all evens out' are thrown at my every move. The wealth of trial preparation and evidence research that is usually used and brought forward in celebrity trials for the frivolous lives of the rich and the famous (Chris Evans, Catherine Zeta-Jones, Michael Barrymore, Chris Tarrant) was not afforded to me.

My trial lasted a mere seven days, not nearly enough for a thorough shot at proving my innocence beyond a shadow of a doubt. My defence lasted a day in trial time. But then again, unlike those who can afford expensive, top-drawer lawyers to help act out their media trials, I was from society's underbelly and I now know from the bottom of my heart how (though not why) it was all done to someone like me.

Every day in prison, the one prevailing thought that gets me up and out of bed in the morning is that of my two boys. They remain my only will to live. I am their mother and I am defiant in my fight to hold on to them and to love them as much as I possibly can. To this day I still maintain a very close relationship with them but it has not been easy, especially since I am so far away. I can only view events from afar instead of actively affect them myself.

Conor and Christy were born in 1993 and 1994 respectively after I had lived with the thought that I could not bear any more children for fourteen years. They were so special to me, a near miracle. I cared about them enough to give up using heroin during my pregnancies, so they would be born clean. Dougie got custody of Conor and Christy but they were eventually taken into care after he admitted he could not cope with raising them. He was not very involved in their parenting and so was forced to attend parenting classes under the close supervision of Social Services. My babies were returned to him after a few months of this. I was in remand in Risley and every other day he would bring the boys to the prison to see me. I was allowed a pitiful five hours with my babies every three weeks. It was just not enough time with them to even try to carry on as normal or to have time to develop and nurture bonds with them. They were far too young to understand what was going on but unfortunately they got used to saying goodbye to their mummy at the end of each visit. It broke my heart each and every single time.

I was moved to a prison in Essex in April 1996 and Dougie would make the journey down to London with the boys to visit me because his brother lived above a pub in Bethnal Green, not a long way from the prison. However, on 21 June 1996, the day before he was supposed to bring the boys to the prison to see me, I phoned the number he gave me at 7.45 p.m. as agreed, ten minutes before night lock-up for me.

Dougie told me he had met someone else in London and that she was going to be the boys' mother. He then put down the phone and took it off the hook. Of course I panicked. I didn't know where my sons were for about a week and I was terrified for them so I phoned Social Services. I was told that I was acting the 'paranoid, absent parent' and they were uncooperative and uncommunicative. I eventually got hold of Dougie a couple of weeks later. When he answered the phone I could clearly hear Conor crying hysterically in the background. When I asked what was wrong, he coldly told me that Conor had been naughty. I tried to make him understand that the boys were not winding him up on purpose and that a two-year-old is just learning and therefore not capable of 'winding him up'. It was unreal. It was arranged between Dougie and me that I would phone to talk to Conor a few times a week. Every time I phoned, I had to listen to Conor crying down the phone to me, telling me that his 'daddy' was hitting him.

I had to get my sons out of that house. I found out from Dougie's mother that he was living with a woman who had had five of her own children taken away from her for neglect and abuse and that he had met her when I was pregnant with Christy. She had had a son around the same time and that son was living with them. I tried to get through to Social Services for a week but the woman who was dealing with my children was always 'in meetings' or 'not in that day' or had gone for a 'home visit'. Basically, every excuse that could be thought of kept me from talking to the social worker in charge in the welfare of my children. I got a sinking feeling in my stomach and it just would not leave.

The next time I spoke to Dougie's mother, she informed me that Social Services had been to visit the children and had removed the woman's son from the household because of neglect and abuse but had left my two sons there. This turned into another ridiculous day when I was not able to get through to the social worker. Dougie's mother then informed me that the police had been by to see Dougie's neighbour because they had seen Conor break an upstairs window and push things through it. When the neighbour had returned home a few hours later, Conor was still by the broken window. The police eventually had to break into the house because every time they knocked or banged on the door, there was no answer. What they found inside was horrifying, especially to me trapped, helpless in prison. They found that Conor and Christy had been locked up in a room together for around ten hours with no adult attention whatsoever. In the bedroom, they found Dougie and the new woman stoned out of their faces in bed.

Even the governor at my prison, Governor Cross, got concerned for the safety of my baby boys once he was played recorded security tapes of my phone calls. He'd called the head of Social Services to inform them that he was sending the tapes to them by courier. If they still did nothing then he would take it upon himself to do something for my babies. Bless Governor Cross because the boys suddenly found themselves back in local-authority care. However, the social worker then informed me that she did not have enough financial resources to take the boys to visit me down in Essex where I was. She also said that it would be a major upset for them to travel the distance. This meant that I would only be able to see them once every six months. That sinking feeling began to grow, threatening to consume me. Luckily, I was transferred to HMP Styal, closer to them and to Manchester.

The day before my next visit with my sons, I was visited by the social worker who had come to ask me to sign a consent form agreeing that my boys be placed into long-term foster care. She held on to one corner of the form and pointed repeatedly to me to sign along the dotted line. I was defiant and adamant that I read everything. I pulled the form from the social worker's hand, saying I wouldn't be signing anything without reading it first. On the front page was written 'Long-term foster care' and underneath, in tiny letters, was 'and adoption'. I lost my temper at this underhanded attempt to get me to consent to losing my children to adoptive parents. I raised my voice, telling her she would have a fight on her hands in a courtroom if she were going to try and have my sons adopted. Then I called over the screw handling the visits and asked him if he had witnessed what had just happened. I asked if he would sign something to verify his presence and what he had witnessed. He said he would be glad to, causing the social worker to walk out on me in a huff. Too right, she wasn't taking my children from me.

I wrote to the head of Social Services, informing her of what had happened and that I would be taking them to court. The reply I received informed me that a different social worker had taken on the boys' case and the boys would be brought up for a six-hour visit the next day. However, the powers that be did not stop at their underhanded attempts to totally mess with my children.

Conor and Christy have been separated ever since going into foster care and are allowed to speak with each other just once a week. They do not have a conference call with me so I am forced to speak to them individually. Somehow Conor knows his mum is innocent though and we happily discuss life when I get out of here. I am repeatedly told to not tell them of my innocence or 'get their hopes up' by discussing my release. In June 1998, I was sent a letter telling me that in order to help prepare the boys for the adoptive process I was only allowed to speak to them once a month, which I completely disagreed with. I speak to them once a week and it is the only time I feel free. The process is so difficult for the boys as well. They are being brainwashed to accept these sneaky divide-and-conquer tactics. They are taken from their mum and now from each other, despite being each other's last hope for a proper family. Conor has developed behavioural difficulties, because he has been shopped around the system away from a stable support structure for so long. Christy barely knows who I am and I think he finds it hard to accept that this voice is in fact his mother. But I will fight on because I know who those children are and what they mean to me. They are part of me, they are my blood and flesh and years of my life and I love them more than I love life. I would give anything to have those years back with them and make it different; to nurture and protect them; help them and love them and watch them grow. But I can't and instead have to fight to get out of here, even though I'm innocent. I want to spend the rest of my life making up for lost time, rebuilding old bonds and loving them like they should be loved.

It was a quick, painless and easy conviction; Sue was inarticulate and did not know how to challenge her conviction. She was someone who would go down without a fight, someone who would simply disappear, swallowed by an unjust system. Sue went to jail, allegedly an innocent woman. Her struggle will not end there and her empowerment has only just begun.

Solicitors did prepare a paper for her appeal. The issue of whether there was a lurking doubt surrounding the conviction was debated. When appealing against conviction, the applicable legal test is whether the conviction is safe. If it is the conviction stands, if not, it must be quashed. This hardly takes into account the humanity behind being wrongfully convicted. However, the issue of lurking doubt was quashed by the chambers that prepared advice to Sue's solicitors. They repeatedly stated that the forensic evidence was too strong despite being able to deconstruct it in practically the same manner that Sue has done.

A separate report exists in Sue's legal papers, written by one Nigel Fieldhouse, which (unqualified as to its source), does go so far as to say that there was

>...no irregularity during the course of the trial and the whole conduct of the trial by the Learned Judge including the summing up was not only meticulous but a model of fairness.

It went on to advise that there would be no grounds for appeal against Sue's conviction. The sheer backslapping in-house solidarity between the judges and the crown and solicitors is without limit sometimes, and where someone who is best forgotten is up for appeal, it is best to trust the instincts of the educated over the rights of the underprivileged. Money will always win, education will always open doors and people like Sue will always be left behind, filling up spaces in jails, to honour industrial contracts for war-monger governments.

Reading through human-rights reports on Third World countries, the most frequent phrase that pops up is that of seditious citizens 'being disappeared' and mass graves being discovered. When it's happening in South America or Sri Lanka or Turkey, it's hard to put faces to these horrific abuses of human dignity. Yet what people don't realise is that these acts happen here, in England, in our own back yards. Around us every day, the police are 'disappearing' people and depositing them in these mass graves, at Her Majesty's pleasure. The prison, the mass grave, consists of countless citizens lost to their families each day, except the reasons are less dignified here than in these other countries. People are not disappeared for disobeying or criticising regimes, nor are they disappeared for religious or cultural oppression. People are disappeared for profit and gross incompetence.

Capitalism is invading the prisons and creating privatised industrial complexes, where, to keep contracts ticking over and corporate boards happy, the cells are filled to busting point. People are 'disappeared' in England practically every day to fill up these jail cells. Anyone can become a target but the easiest are those living on the lowest income level, those who have no voice, no education to find the confidence to fight, and no money to buy their way back into society. No one will miss them. Especially junkie-prostitutes. Who wants them around anyway? Sullying our estates and making our street corners look sleazy and bad. Hide them away, fill those cells, they can't fight back. That is where Sue is. Lost in a system that needs her only as a statistic. While on the other end of the scale, her children are being used as a negative statistic. There is no account taken of the sheer emotion and gut-wrenching powerless horror at being taken away from your mother, your child, your family.

If and when you are returned to each other, one of you has evolved while the other has stayed in stasis. You don't recognise each other any more. Your relationship has missed out on so many important moments and developments that there is nothing left for you at all. Sue fights to hold on to her kids and still have an emotional impact in their lives, because without that they forget who she is, and once they forget who she is, *she* will forget who she is. And she could be anyone. Yet, the system has made her a no-one. No one visits her or writes to her. Her only friends are inmates and her only passion is the memory of her children and the knowledge of her innocence. She clings to her innocence like a badge of honour because the moment she lets go of that is the moment the system's 'rehabilitation' process makes its first victory on her and the brainwashing begins. But she won't let that happen. Sue can prove her innocence to anyone with the time to listen and the space for open-minded thought. Giving her the support she needs is the only thing that can help her unify with her children once more and soon.

Keith Li

April 2003, HMP Long Lartin

I was convicted of kidnapping and joint-enterprise murder, along with five other people, at Manchester Crown Court on 3 July 1996 and sentenced to life imprisonment. Up until the day I was convicted I had faith in the British justice system, believing that there was no way I could be blamed for something I did not do and had *nothing* to do with. I have tried to put my story together here, in the hope that people out there will help me prove my innocence. I have always considered myself a strong individual and I have never been afraid to face up to the consequences of my own actions. I am not too arrogant to admit when I am wrong but I can be stubborn when I know I am right. If I had anything to do with this crime, I assure you I would have been the first to accept the lesser charge of manslaughter that was offered to me by the prosecution, throughout the trial. Had I done so, I am informed, I would have been home three years ago. Many see the stance I have chosen as being naïve, but I believe that a man should stand up for his rights and not cower in the face of injustice.

At my trial I was accused of being a Triad boss in Manchester – even though there was no corroborating evidence whatsoever to substantiate this damaging allegation. I have no criminal history – indeed I come from a reputable family. All of my family work for legitimate businesses. I was born in Hong Kong and by the time I was sixteen I had already travelled quite extensively throughout Europe and some parts of Asia. My last travels were cut short due to my father's ill health and I returned to England in 1992 as a result. I was twenty-five years old and went into business with my brother. We opened a chip shop together in Lymm, Cheshire. I had recently got married and went on to have two children.

It was while at this chip shop that I met Be Keung and his friends who later became my co-accused. Be Keung was hired to work for the business and his friends (Sil Sin, Wah Tai, John Wong and Eddie Leung) sometimes hung around the shop, waiting for him, etc. I never went out with them socially or otherwise at this stage.

Something that I am ashamed of but which has to be told is that I had an affair with a woman called Lily Lau in 1993. I had met her through Be Keung who had recommended her as a prospective employee due to a shortage of staff. She started working at the chip shop and a relationship developed between us. She became pregnant and demanded that I leave my wife – I refused. She eventually decided to have an abortion. I supported her decision and accompanied her to all the medical appointments but could not be there at the time of the operation due to pressing family commitments. She was furious and broke up with me, ending our relationship.

In 1994 I left the chip shop. I had decided to open a restaurant in Preswich, Manchester. To my surprise Lily Lau got back in contact, offering to work and help out at the restaurant. I accepted her help and our relationship started up again. Not long after opening the restaurant I received a phone call from someone claiming to be a member of the Triads. This person on the phone said that he was calling on behalf of his boss Simon. He demanded that I pay them £500 a week for protection. I refused. I didn't take the phone call too seriously because I'd never been intimidated in this way before. Also I've always felt able to look after myself due to having trained in martial arts from an early age.

The restaurant business turned out to be a disaster. After a short period of time custom just seemed to dry up. I decided to cut my losses and shut down the restaurant after the Christmas period. My family travelled back to Hong Kong around this time and I was going to rent out our house and tie up the business before going back to join them. The police should have documents on their files which prove this was my intention because I had estate agents' documents about arranging the letting of the house and my ex-wife would verify that I was due to return to Hong Kong to join them.

Towards the end of December 1994, a week or so before I was due to close the restaurant for good, I was surprised by Be Keung and his friends turning up. I hadn't seen them since leaving the chip shop in Lymm. They'd heard that I was closing the place down and going back to Hong Kong. They offered to help me pack up and move out and also asked me to give them self-defence lessons while I was still in England. I agreed. The restaurant landlord was going to take at least a month to return my deposit so I was going to be in England for a while longer anyway.

I closed the restaurant at the beginning of January 1995. In mid-January Be Keung and Sil Sin came round to see me. Sil Sin asked me to help him with a matter he was trying to resolve. He told me that he had been burgled while away on holiday in Hong Kong. He believed that his two flatmates were responsible as well as some friends of theirs. Sil Sin lived in a shared student house but had padlocked his bedroom door before going away. I agreed to speak to the people involved and help him sort it out if I could. He was distraught and I thought I could help.

When we got there his flatmates admitted they'd been up to no good. I simply told them that we could resolve the matter by them returning the stolen property or they could pay Sil Sin the value of the items stolen so that he could replace them. If not, I said we could call the police and let them sort it out. They agreed to sort it out amongst themselves. I mention all this because I was later falsely accused of 'demanding money with menaces and threatening behaviour' – this is ridiculous. I did not threaten these people in any way, other than 'threatening' to call the police if need be, and they even admitted that this was the case to the police.

My brother-in-law is a chef and had come up from London to work with me at the restaurant. When I closed the restaurant I told him I would help him move his things back to London. We did this on 27 January 1995 and I thought I would take the opportunity while in the south of England, of going to France for a couple of days with Lily. She thought it was a good idea and when Be Keung, Sil Sin and Wah Tai found out they also wanted to come. Lily didn't mind so I hired a car, figuring that we could go to Paris and Sil Sin would help drive some of the way.

When we got to France Sil Sin wouldn't do any driving, saying he felt uncomfortable driving on the right-hand side of the road, so we changed plans, not going to Paris and instead drove round the Calais area. We parked up in Calais and decided to split up for a few hours. Before we did, Be Keung said he was a bit strapped for cash and asked me if he could borrow £200. I had no problem lending it to him. When we met up again Be Keung said he'd bought a gun. I thought this was a little strange but he told me he'd wanted to buy it as a present for a friend of his who had recently joined a gun club in North Manchester. So I didn't question it. I figured the gun would be bought legally and registered so there shouldn't be a problem. I never saw the gun myself because it was gift-wrapped. I was later accused of being 'an evil genius' by going to France for the sole purpose of buying this gun. Surely anyone that wanted to buy a gun to go and murder someone would buy one *illegally* which would be harder to trace? And would buy it more discreetly, without going all the way to France, via customs, with a whole bunch of friends, girlfriend included?

We spent the rest of the day there and returned to England in the evening. The next day I'd arranged to go to Belfast to meet a good friend of mine. I wanted to say goodbye to him personally before I went back to Hong Kong. Be Keung and Sil Sin said they had never been to Ireland before and asked to come. Again I didn't have a problem with it. We stayed there for four days – at the trial it was alleged that I'd been to see my Triad boss and somehow made the other two come with me! This can be proven to be another false and ridiculous claim.

On 9 February at around three in the morning Be Keung and his friends came to my house. I was asleep and could hardly believe it when I opened the door to find Be Keung there – his face was covered in blood. He said he'd been beaten up by a group of lads. He mentioned some names, one of them being the deceased, Eddie Hui. He said he didn't know why he had been beaten up but that they'd said they were Triads and that he was really scared. This was the first time I had ever heard of the deceased.

Be Keung was terrified to the point that he asked me to help him. I felt sorry for him and although I didn't want to get involved I agreed to take him to London and find him a job so that he could be safe from whoever had done this to him. Be Keung was so scared that he insisted on leaving for London immediately that same night – about four o'clock in the morning – but when we reached Birmingham he changed his mind. He told me he couldn't just go without sorting things out with his sister in Manchester first so we drove back.

Be Keung stayed at my house that day and the next day all his friends came to my house: Sil Sin, Wah Tai, John Wong and Eddie Leung. They all showed concern and told me then about someone they knew called Tony Fu. They said if they talked to him they'd be able to get to the bottom of why Be Keung was beaten up. Be Keung asked me to accompany them to make sure they all didn't get beaten up. So we drove to Manchester and found this guy Tony Fu. Fu said he could probably find out where one of the guys who'd beaten up Be Keung lived and he willingly agreed to accompany us to try and find him (Eddie Hui). He spent the rest of the afternoon and evening with us. During that time we went shopping, went to a restaurant to eat, and generally hung out in many different public places. Eventually we got an address for the lad Be Keung was looking for. Fu had phoned a friend who'd told him where this lad was. We drove past the Golden Arch Chip Shop in Glossop where Eddie Hui worked and as the shop was busy with customers decided to return at closing time. We passed time by driving to Manchester Airport and back, stopping for coffee there. When we went back Be Keung decided he was too scared to confront the guy so after five or ten minutes we left.

On the 11 February, the day of the murder, Be Keung and Sil Sin came to my house in the afternoon and both said that they wanted to go to London that night. At about eight o'clock we went to eat at a restaurant called Quincy's in Didsbury, then we went across the road to the Dog and Partridge Pub (at about 9.15 p.m.) to wait for Wah Tai and John Wong to meet up with us. We'd planned to travel to London together and I still planned to help Be Keung find a job there. I don't think it was just the fact that he'd been beaten up by Triads. I think lots of things generally had already been getting him down at this time. Girlfriend issues, family issues, work and the like. He wanted a break and some distance for a while before he came back to deal with everything.

They arrived about half an hour after we did. We stayed in the pub until the end of the Manchester United v Manchester City football match which was being shown live on TV. I'd had a few drinks but I distinctly remember a bald-headed man who I'm pretty sure made comments about the fact that there were 'five Chinese men' drinking in his pub and would've remembered us. There was also a woman in there, quite flirty around us. I'm positive she would have remembered us.

We left for London very soon after the match finished and stopped at Knutsford Services on the M6 so I could get some coffee. John Wong and Wah Tai went up to the restaurant to buy food while the rest of us went to play on the gaming machines. While there we witnessed an argument between a man and the manageress of the place. I was later told that the argument was over the change machine giving incorrect change. The manageress logged this argument and the police later took a statement from this man. We continued on our journey to London. I remember stopping at services on the M1 to sleep and we got to London the next morning.

I spent the next couple of weeks seeing friends and going out. On 2 March Lily Lau came down to see me from Manchester. She was worried and told me that the police wanted to see me in relation to the murder of the deceased and that they believed I'd done it. She also told me that I'd been set up by the Triads and should leave the country, taking her with me. I told her I wasn't going to run from something I hadn't done. I immediately wanted to go back to Manchester to see the police, sort it out and clear my name from any accusations. I told all my co-accused what was going on and said that we had better go back to Manchester. I asked them to come but they didn't want to because they were scared of both the Triads and the police. It was up to them but I said Sil Sin had to come as he used his credit card for the car hire. We went straight back to Manchester the next day, 3 March 1995, in the hope of clearing it up. On the way we got stuck in traffic. It was getting past 5.30 p.m. so I phoned the car-hire company and asked them to wait for me to return the car. When we arrived at the premises the police were waiting.

I had the muzzle of a gun forced against my head with an officer threatening to 'blow my head off'. They cuffed me across the back of my head with the gun a number of times. I was in a state of shock and confusion, bleeding by now and I remember seeing Sil Sin's face cut. After hitting me they stood on my wrist and my back, kicking me and slapping me a few times. This was after they had me on the floor face down and double-cuffed.

A doctor examined me after I got transferred from Manchester to Buxton Police Station. The doctors said I was okay and gave me a couple of pills for the pain but when a new desk sergeant came on duty and saw me he felt the need to recall the doctor. The back of my head had swollen up. I still get pain from the injuries nine years on.

While in custody I was given a solicitor and he advised me to tell the police everything I knew, which I fully complied with. I believed that the police would check out what I'd told them and then let me go. But then I discovered that they weren't going to bother. Later on, one of the policemen came to my cell and admitted that he knew I was being stitched up but unless I could tell them why these people would go to so much trouble to 'get me' I would be taking the blame for the murder.

I told the police again and again that I really didn't

know why or who was stitching me up. If I did I would have told them, I had nothing to lose but the police didn't believe me. Some time later they even suggested I should say that my co-accused committed the murder and that I only helped them on the getaway route after this happened. I told them I couldn't do that as it did not happen and would be a lie. None of my co-accused could possibly have committed the murder. I know this for a fact because we were all at Knutsford Services at the time. As far as I know no one bothered to check through any CCTV footage which could have cleared us.

According to the police the murder took place at 11 p.m. and an independent witness also verified this. A man local to the area passed by the crime scene on the way to pick up his wife and says he saw two men running out. He was forced to stop his car because two men ran in front of it from the direction of the chip shop. He said they then ran down the side of his car before jumping over a wall and disappearing into the darkness. He was certain of the time because he was picking up his wife and also because when he'd picked her up, he saw the ambulance going to the chip shop. The description he gave of the two men did not match any of us. I do not know why but this person did not appear in court nor was his statement mentioned in court. Surely this was pertinent to my case. There were no forensics linking us to the crime either.

The man who had the argument with the manageress at Knutsford Services made a statement claiming that when he went into the gaming area he saw three Chinese men playing on the machines, then two more Chinese men came to join them from the restaurant area upstairs. The description he gave matched us closely. He said he'd watched us play on the machines for about fifteen minutes before deciding to play himself. In his statement he said he saw us at about 11.25 p.m. His argument with the manageress had been logged at 11.35 p.m. After he'd watched us playing, he wanted to play the machines himself. He'd gone and put a £20 note into the change machine and it subsequently malfunctioned. If you measure the time it takes to get from the chip shop in Glossop to Knutsford Services, there is no way we could have got there in that time if we'd left around 11 p.m. It's impossible. Yet the crown's case was that I 'sent' or 'ordered' John Wong and Wah Tai to go and kill this guy Eddie and then meet up with the rest of us at the services. This is not true – we were all at the services together so they couldn't have murdered the deceased. This statement wasn't mentioned in court nor did this witness appear.

A man (who I now believe to be a police informer) was placed in a cell with Wong after he'd been arrested. He claimed Wong had bragged to him about the shooting, saying he'd shot Eddie Hui because he owed him money. He also said that Wong claimed to have shot the deceased three or four times, and was the boss of his gang! According to the police, the deceased had been shot once only. This statement was never mentioned in court nor did this person appear.

On one of the occasions during a pre-trial hearing at Buxton Magistrates' Court, Wong was kept in a holding cell. Also in this cell was another prisoner. I became the topic of a conversation between them. Wong allegedly told him that he was charged with a murder that he hadn't committed but that he was going to admit to it. When this man asked him why he would do something that stupid, Wong had replied that he'd made a deal and would only get eight years. By chance this man was remanded to the prison I was in and when he'd realised I was there he made contact. He told me of the conversation that had taken place and said that he'd contacted me because he believed

Wong was trying to set an innocent man up, which went against his code of ethics. I told my solicitor this and she asked me to ask this man if he would be willing to make an official statement. He did and the statement was made about twelve months before the trial. Yet again, this witness was not called to give evidence nor was his statement brought up in court.

The trial started with the prosecution reading a statement given by Tony Fu. On 16 February he'd voluntarily approached the police and made a statement to the effect that he had been kidnapped. Less than a week afterwards he left the country. The court admitted Fu's evidence even though he didn't turn up in court. He said that my co-accused and me had *kidnapped* him and made him tell us where the deceased worked. He said he was a Triad and conveniently left out of his statement the fact that we'd driven together to the chip shop in Glossop and back via the airport. Why was this evidence allowed in court when no one could cross-examine him? We went shopping and hung around plenty of public places. There's proof of this from receipts – and probably CCTV footage too. He spent plenty of time on his own when he could have run away if he'd wanted. He'd met us in a public place in Manchester with loads of people around at the time and in broad daylight. How could we have taken him against his will and how come the police couldn't find one single person who could verify such allegations?

Tony Fu also claimed to be a member of the Wo Sing Wo Triads so surely whatever he said was in order to protect his own interests according to his own agenda? If he were a Triad then naturally he wouldn't admit that he'd voluntarily helped us find the whereabouts of his gang friend, the deceased. He'd be worried about the consequences. He'd be in trouble with his gang and the police would probably have added him to their list of 'murderers' too.

Why was Tony Fu kept away from the trial? Prior to my appeal hearing, the prosecution decided to disclose to the defence a number of documents that had not been disclosed at the time of my trial. They included an internal Derbyshire Police report dated 17 March 1995 that indicated a blacked-out address for Tony Fu in Hong Kong that may have been an old address. There was a letter dated 27 June 1995 from Derbyshire Police to the Hong Kong Police seeking confirmation of Fu's address in Hong Kong, but asking that 'any checks be done covertly'. Then there was Document 256, a message dated 9 August 1995 from Derbyshire Police to Hong Kong Police. It confirmed that Fu had entered Hong Kong on 22 February 1995 and indicated a blacked-out address for him. It also said, 'We cannot do a covert confirmation of him being there due to the isolation and nature of the village. If you wish a confirmation done, we would have to approach the address direct.'

The document also records Derbyshire Police's reply: 'Do nothing further.'

This evidence, suppressed at the time of my trial, shows that had the prosecution chosen to bring him to court they could have done so.

While in custody I was given some paperwork to my case. It included a number of statements Lily Lau made to the police. They'd arrested her on 23 February, released her and then arrested her again on 27 April. With each fresh statement she made, Lily's story changed more and more towards the police version. She started off claiming that I would never do anything like that and that I wasn't a Triad, to hearing me plan the whole thing. She said that the police had advised her that unless she gave evidence against me and became a prosecution witness, they would charge her with the importation of a firearm and maybe even murder.

In court she said that she'd seen me go out and get the gun cartridges on the weekend we came back from France. But I was in Belfast and this could be proved. John Wong and Wah Tai claimed that I sent them to steal cartridges from a gun club. How can two different stories be acceptable?

The prosecution case ended after we were offered the plea of manslaughter if we all agreed to take it. My QC told me that if I pleaded guilty to a manslaughter charge he could guarantee no life sentence and a maximum fixed term of between ten to fifteen years. He also said that if I didn't take it, the judge would slam me. I refused the offer and the trial continued.

Sil Sin gave evidence after me and his version of events was so contradictory that even the judge seemed to lose patience with him. He purported to being terrified of me and too scared to refuse being involved and was pressured to use his car as a getaway vehicle. Apparently I'd also ordered him to burn his car after the murder to destroy the evidence. Under cross-examination (his car hadn't been burnt) he said he'd not wanted to. These actions are not consistent with his previous claims of being terrified of me. Everything he said was absolute rubbish – and forensics proved there wasn't anything in the car to show that it had been a murderer's getaway car.

I know I have been set up to be blamed for the crime and Lily Lau confirmed as much to me when she came down to London to see me the day before I was arrested. I believe she was threatened to say the things she did – partly by the police and partly by the Triads. But I still don't know why I was set up. My affairs with Lily Lau and the fact that I refused to pay protection money to a bunch of thugs seems scant justification for being put in this position. I cannot understand why my co-accused felt it was okay to take the blame for someone else's vicious actions and accept 'deals' when surely nothing less than freedom and a clear name is a God-given right for those who have not committed crimes?

I have now been in jail for nine years. I hope one day soon that I'll be able to prove I was totally innocent of this crime. The truth has to endure because in spite of the consequences I am still not prepared to admit guilt or plead guilty to something I did not do. However, I have learnt to be pragmatic about my sentence too. I got twenty-years-life for murder and five years for kidnap to run concurrent. At the appeal, among many other arguments, it was submitted that Tony Fu's statement should have been excluded on the basis of Article 6 (3) (d) of the European Convention of Human Rights. This confers a right on a person charged with a criminal offence 'to examine or have examined witnesses against him'. The judge dismissed this article 'as an extra string to the bow in relation to the absence of any opportunity on the part of the defendant to cross-examine'.

6

THE RELEASED

Rob Brown

> This is my true confession not a prisoner's poetic
> quip
> This pen is in the hands of the writer and not
> some detective's grip
> I was wrapped in peaceful slumber when they
> came to take me away
> I got captured in a nightmare, that is still going
> on today
> As my trial has never ended and I fought a lonely
> campaign
> Still you judge and condemn with a stroke of your
> pen as to you it's all the same.
> I was abused and humiliated by what seemed like
> a posse of men
> I was asked so many questions of how and where
> and when
> I was told to do step-ups on a chair, legally naked
> and scared

My vulnerability seemed to amuse the detectives
    who stood and stared
And it did not matter what I said, they would
    twist it that's for sure
The physical and physiological tactics was
    something I could not endure.
One said 'Sign a statement, son' or continue this
    little caper
So for reasons of self-preservation, I added my
    signature to paper.
But the trial was something else, man, some kind
    of judicial act
Convicted on manufactured evidence that is
    inconsistent with fact
Now the time erodes in prison and it's gone
    another decade
But there is no deterrent for an innocent man
    when justice is but a charade.

I first set eyes upon Robert Brown on the morning of 13 November 2002, rushing from Temple tube to the Royal Courts of Justice to attend his appeal. Rob had been in prison since May 1977. From the day he was convicted in October 1977, he had steadfastly refused to admit any moral responsibility for the crime and had instead fought a lonely campaign to clear his name of the murder for which he had been blamed, a quarter of a century ago.

I pulled open the door to the appeal court that day to find a room packed with assorted people: family, friends, campaigners, press, the odd law student and a whole bunch of legal figures. Conscious of paper shuffling and the muffled movements of a hushed yet restless audience, I snuck in as quietly as I could and squashed onto the end of a bench, taking in the scene around me. My eyes were immediately drawn to the figure sitting in the cage at the front left side of the courtroom. I tried not to stare but my eyes kept wandering back to him every few minutes. Rob Brown was impeccably dressed in a dark suit and sat upright, listening intently to the judge. Lord Justice Rose read monotonously from a manuscript, losing his place every so often.

Greater Manchester Police arrested me in May 1977 for the non-payment of a £75 fine. I was nineteen years old. At the police station they asked me if I'd been questioned about the murder of a woman called Annie Walsh, to which I replied no. The police took me upstairs and I was punched heavily in the abdomen. I fell down on the floor and was grabbed by the hair and thrown back into a chair. They told me that I would get this treatment for as long as I kept replying to them like I was doing. I proceeded to be physically and psychologically tortured by these men for forty-eight hours – at one stage they took all my clothes off me for forensics, and forced me to do step-ups on a chair, completely naked, while punching and slapping me. I was extremely frightened and just couldn't handle them in my naïve, uneducated state. By the end of it I would have confessed and signed my name to anything to make it all stop. No matter what I said, the police refused to believe me and constantly distorted what I was saying. They were evil. The last thing they were prepared to do was to listen to anything I had to say. They just wanted to mock, beat, threaten and intimidate me and enjoyed doing it.

I had never met or heard of Annie Walsh or any of her family before that day. I'd moved to a Manchester council estate from Glasgow in a bid to make a fresh start of my life. My father used to beat my ma up and when I was nine, for my own safety, my ma had me placed into an orphanage. I lived there until I was sixteen and then went home again. I intervened one night when my father was beating up my ma and the next morning my father came into my bedroom, told me to pack my bag and leave. So I did and went to Manchester. That orphanage gave me some of the happiest times of my life. That place is the reason I didn't grow up with ignorance, like racism, sexism, violence or anything else. I went back to visit recently after getting out.

The police concocted a statement that said things like I'd helped Annie Walsh carry her bags home and she'd invited me in for tea and biscuits. She'd then caught me trying to steal her bag and I'd panicked and killed her. The statement was a load of lies and had no real fact in it. I believed it impossible that I could be found guilty of a capital offence of murder when there was absolutely no evidence apart from an uncorroborated confession, just words on a piece of paper. I later discovered that £213 had been left untouched in Annie Walsh's handbag, which had been left on the kitchen table. When you look at the details of the murder, it's obvious the police theory was nothing but a sick joke. The murder took place on 28 January 1977 but I wasn't arrested until nearly four months after, in May.

In March that year a witness, Margaret Jones, picked out a thirty-seven-year-old man in an identity parade who had a harelip. His name was Robert James Hill and the police also found a fibre on his coat that matched in colour and microscopic detail to fibres found on the victim's clothes. So there was a strong case against this man. But the police let him go and suppressed the evidence against him. The same witness identified me in a parade on 18 May and said that I looked like the same man. So her identification was obviously unreliable because I was nineteen years old and he was thirty-seven years old so there's no equation of age there.

At my trial the prosecution had the audacity to bring out a pair of bloodstained jeans and show them to the jury. They had absolutely no evidence to convict me with other than the police statement against me so they stooped to bringing out these jeans. They were proven to be totally irrelevant to either Annie Walsh or myself and actually belonged to a woman who had suffered a miscarriage. But their dirty tricks worked and the jeans were used as a tendentious ploy to produce an efficacious effect in the eyes and the minds of the jurors. Even though the judge said, 'We all know the jeans are irrelevant,' mentally, the jury had already connected me to bloodstained clothes. Can you imagine what a nineteen-year-old boy would have felt like? I was fucking terrified and I remember screaming at the top of my lungs to the victim's family that I was innocent. I didn't do it. It was totally surreal because I thought that the court would realise that there'd been a mistake, step in and let me go. If not then, then the next day or the day after that. How could they not realise – not one person in that whole system of people – what they'd done? This was my state of mind for twelve whole months after I got convicted because I was so sure someone from the court system would know that they'd convicted an innocent person because of the police. I had to grow up pretty quickly after that and get a grip on myself.

When I went into jail, all I could possibly say to anyone was who I was. I'm innocent. I never did it. You can't tell it any other way than the way it is when you're innocent. I proclaimed my innocence to everybody I met. In the shower, cleaning my teeth, slopping out, whatever. People got sick of me and they didn't want to hear it. I couldn't stop saying it because it was the truth. I wasn't articulate though because I never got an education. For ten years I screamed out that I was innocent and then I realised that the only way to get people to listen was to educate myself and prove my innocence. So that's what I started to do. And by default I learnt to truly understand myself. I used to bang myself up into isolation and read: Sartre, Anais Nin, Victor Hugo, Germaine Greer, Alexandre Dumas, everything I could get my hands on, to give myself an insight into the feminine side of me, the masculine side of me, who I was, where I was, to discover yourself in a little black hole in the ground where there's nothing else. You can't turn right and you can't turn left and there's no out and there's no in. You're just there in the middle of a hole. That's where I was and I had to dissect myself, every little part of me, to know every little part of me. No one knows me better than I know myself – nobody could possibly know me because of what I went through.

You have to know yourself better than anybody to survive prison and come out at the CA. You have to know your weaknesses and you have to know your strengths. You have to know how far you can push it to the limit. You have to know who the enemy is or you have lost the fight because in some respects it's an unseen enemy. It's like, what is the only positive thing that prison can give you if you're innocent? Time. What you do with it is up to you, but it's always there. You can educate yourself and become articulate and form highly educated opinions on subjects or you can take drugs and rot, or you can keep yourself to yourself, in stasis, and slowly go crazy with this weird pressure and learn nothing – dwell on all your failings instead. They're plotting against you every day, prison officers, probation officers and psychologists, all trying to make you paranoid and playing head games with you, trying to brainwash you into submission, and sink you into fresh depths of sadness and despair. You're expected to feel guilty for smoking a joint and for following your own faith.

Some people become stunted; they don't continue to grow in some aspects of things. They might grow mentally, but they might remain stunted emotionally, sexually or spiritually. A lot of innocent people give up inside and don't even admit it to themselves. They lose the empowerment to fight for righteous freedom. They're too scared to believe in concepts of freedom any more because they lose the belief that they'll ever get out. The so-called justice system put them there – everything they ever lived by. They harbour negative feelings that they don't even understand – in prison everyone's got their own problems, it's up to you whether you exercise your mind or let it stay stagnant, ignorant and uncommunicative or aggressive, or angry. The depths of my anger and my frustration almost destroyed me.

I knew what the officers were capable of. I saw them do it to people throughout my sentence. They did it to me. Kicked my four front teeth out and broke my ribs. Some of it I deserved, some of it I never. You fight for your own life and you lose the plot for a while. Then you start fighting it with all these little strengths as you become more articulate and educated. You begin to open little compartments within yourself: spiritually, emotionally and physically. Even physiologically because the stress you're living with everyday can do you damage.

I used to use anger and aggression and shout and scream at the screws and try and attack them. They could laugh at and deal with that – because all I knew was pain and hostility, and the people running the prison system are experts at that. All I knew was anger; I forgot about love or kindness or warmth. I couldn't deal with it in there. That was me going through the first ten years of my sentence from a nineteen-year-old boy to a thirty-year-old man. It was like a screw would walk by, smoking a fag, and say something like, 'Did you watch the football last night?' And whereas before I would tell them all to fuck off, as I became more articulate, I would say, 'Look I don't want to talk to you about football. Why don't you come and read my case papers? I'm innocent.' They couldn't deal with me then. Anger they can deal with. Reasonable logic? No chance.

I thought to myself, why am I wasting my energy, screaming at them on a daily basis? So when they used to talk to me I used to come out of my cell and turn my back on them because they wouldn't reason with me and look at my papers. They thought I was a contentious, obnoxious little bastard. I knew different. I had been buried alive in a hell-shaped room just filled with emptiness and nothingness. I lived my life from day to day and never stuck pictures on my wall like other inmates did. I never made my cell homely. I would smash the cell up in anger year after year.

When I got to Cat C they didn't know how to take me and said that my file read like a bad novel: he's deranged, delusional, he's in denial. I used to say to them, in denial? What's that, a fucking Egyptian river? And they didn't know how to handle me. If I got involved in an altercation with a screw I wouldn't back off – ever. But if I was wrong about it, I would go back to that screw, with or without other inmates, and say, hey, gov, I just thought about that and I'm sorry. I was wrong. I shouldn't have done that or I shouldn't have said that. A lot of inmates wouldn't do that because they wouldn't accept any responsibility whatsoever even when they were wrong – like I said, some people become stunted and won't grow up. But if I were right about something? I would fight it every little point. Legally or physically I would take the screws on. Obviously I was outnumbered and only weighed eight stone so I wasn't a big guy.

The screws gave me a lot of brutality especially after my first ten years, from 1987–99. They dehumanised and animalised me. After I'd recover from being beaten up I would throw buckets of shit over them and hit them with table legs from behind in protest. But I would never assault a prison officer or an inmate unless I had been assaulted first; it was like I had to wear a coat of armour around me. I would get beaten more and shipped all round to places like Winson Green and Lincoln Segregation. They could ship me out to somewhere and nobody knew where I was and they'd just beat me. There'd be no phones and of course letters I wrote wouldn't get out. Until the bruises went away no one would know where you were and then you'd get shipped back to where you came from. In 1990 my ma wrote to the Home Office asking where I was. They told her they'd never heard of me. I'd done ten years and my ma had visited me every single prison I went to and then all of a sudden she couldn't find me. Can you imagine what that did to my ma? It wasn't just me doing the life sentence it was my ma too.

When you go to prison, you have to be guilty of something. Their logic is that if you're guilty of one thing, you must be guilty of every fucking thing. So if you get nicked and you go in front of the governor, it's a foregone conclusion before you've started. I had something like 290-odd adjudications in twenty-five years – that's off the Richter scale for a lifer. Lifers didn't get nicked, you had to walk that line. Other innocent lifers just gave up. When they'd come and get me and tell me I was working in the textile shop, I wouldn't go to work. I used to tell them to fuck off, do what they want, nick me, I didn't care. After ten years I used to politely say no thank you. The screws would say, 'Excuse me?'

I would say, 'I do not want a job. I never asked for a job. There's millions unemployed. Give a job to someone who wants a fucking job. I would shut the cell door, say thank you and that was it.

They didn't know how to deal with a rational train of thought. Violence, yes, language, no.

On another occasion some of the inmates (myself included) were wolf-whistling and shouting abuse at one of the screws. He was black but we weren't taunting him because he was black and we weren't shouting racist abuse. None of us were racists, in fact we were all friends with black inmates in the prison. We were taunting him because he'd looked down at us from the third-floor landing one day and said, 'Nah, nah, nah nah nah, I'm going home tonight.' He'd goaded us just to show off in front of a female auxiliary working there. Well that's the worse thing you could say to a bunch of cons – especially one who's innocent.

When I got nicked my file read, 'Racist abuse. Every time Brown walks past me he makes racist comments.' I pleaded not guilty on adjudication so the governor said to me, 'Do you disagree with any of the evidence?'

I said, 'Yes, I disagree with all of it because I'm not a racist.' I was in jail for twenty-five years and not one of the screws and not one governor had any clue about who I was or my levels of intelligence. Then the governor said, 'Do you want to ask any questions?' So I said to the governor, 'Yeah. Ask your officer what one of the definitions of the word nigger is in the *Oxford Concise English Dictionary.* The governor replied, 'I'm not asking one of my officers that, Brown.'

So I said, 'Well that's the question I want answered. It's not a racist question, why are you turning it into one?' Basically he didn't want to ask the officer my question because he was black. Yet being a nigger has fuck all to do with being black.

The governor's gone and put his head down because he couldn't look me in the eye, and he's said, 'A black man. A nigger is a black man. Are you satisfied with that, Brown?' He thought that I was asking the question just to get a little argument going about colour, or racism, or just to defend myself. So I said, 'No, I'm not satisfied with that answer, governor.' It just goes to show you what an ignorant man he was. 'Governor,' I said, 'the definition of nigger is "one who is discriminated against". Therefore there's just one nigger among us and as it happens, I am the fucking nigger here.' The governor literally had me thrown back into the cells, yelling all the way, 'Get him outta here!' They don't like being put in their place.

On other occasions when I'd be up in front of the governor, I would say in my defence, 'No comment.' Behaviour in prison? 'No comment.' What do you have to say about the matter? 'No comment.' The governor would say, 'Are you going to sit there and tell me no comment all night?' 'No comment.' The governor would explode and tell me to fuck off and get out. See, I learnt that it takes two to play, so I stopped playing, and stopped speaking to screws. I wasted my time trying to communicate with moronic screws and just lost myself in the process – so with crystal-clear clarity one day I stopped talking to them and was a lot better for it.

I took it every phase and when I wanted to do something I would pack my kit and go down to the screws, knock on the door and say, 'Get me in the block.' I used to put myself in the punishment block and just stay there for twelve months and write. That way I could avoid the prison politics, and all the bullshit, the macho men and being caught up in the violence and the rat race of it all. The whole environment in itself is a really weird and abnormal environment, it really is. Even the screws can't handle the pressure of walking about the landings.

When you consider how long prisons have been around, it is staggering that those in authority still do not have the faintest idea of how to rehabilitate anyone. Prison is not a deterrent for anybody. They tried the short fucking shock treatment and that didn't work. Now everyone has to face these psychologists, as well as prison officers and probation officers. In 1977 the prison system had very few psychologists. They had them but they were in a minority and they didn't keep files on prisoners. It was all done on a confidential basis. After a lot of these paedophile groups took place they started forming psychological profiling. In 1991, 1992, profiling was very avant-garde, the time of Colin Stagg's case. It was very fashionable in the pseudo-psychological world. I would watch them all scoring little points off each other because they thought they were so clever. Fools. They didn't even know that I was in prison for something I never did. I could stand up in the face of a lie and adversity, when the whole system was trying to systematically break my resolve and condition me into accepting moral responsibility for the crime and still speak the truth. The reason they couldn't break my resolve and condition me was because I was innocent. If they had known it I would have spoken to and communicated with them. But there was no point. They used to say, 'We know you're protesting your innocence and we can't get involved with that.' Why? I was just a vulnerable, lonely, totally lost kid when I went in and these so-called upstanding civil servants couldn't listen to my pleas for help because it wasn't in their job description?

Prison psychologists used to call me in for their reports. Well, all I can be is guilty or innocent but they can't reason with evidence, facts or logic. A lot of people went through the motions and said I'd never get out. Prison officers used to come round in the morning and say, 'Morning, Brown. Still here then? Why don't you play the game, lad?' I'd reply, 'Don't fucking patronise me and talk to me like some stupid punk. You can't condition me to accept injustice. You cannot punish me any more.'

You can't force someone to learn something that they don't want to learn. You can't force someone to do something they don't want to do because that's coercion. As a method, that's got nothing to do with rehabilitation or freedom. That's blackmail. So the system, when they brought all these courses in, promoted psychology within the prison system, to justify wasting taxpayers' money and to promote the careers of psychologists who are selling the product themselves.

Psychology departments now have the biggest say in what goes on in the prison system. I really question that. That really frightens me because they have absolute autonomy to get a man, sit him down in a chair, ask him about his crime, and individually at the end of it, say, 'I recommend closed conditions in Cat A or Cat B prisons, a sex-offenders' treatment programme and a cognitive self-change programme,' and then write the reasons for why he or she thinks he needs it. While that's being evaluated and assessed and recommended, that's all on file. If the prisoner decides not to do the courses he will not get the chance to be released on licence as a lifer. The argument is very simple. What if there is no offending behaviour to address, as hundreds of miscarriages of justice have and continue to prove?

You cannot teach or rehabilitate people by saying to them, 'We're going to recommend you for this course. If you don't take this course you will not be considered for parole or home leave. Goodbye.' What do these psychologists really know about life? Some of them are twenty-four, twenty-five years old and have never lived. They come straight out of college with this textbook-theory bullshit. How many have studied behaviour in prison? I was guilty because it said it on my file. They've got to follow the file because they're only doing a job. I was kept in prison because psychologists weren't allowed to tell the truth, even if they were aware of it. A few did and got sacked for it. Those who did the sacking got promoted.

If psychologists cannot tell the truth and if their opinions can only be subjective, how can they be objective? Without any foundation of truth? It's impossible. If there is no foundation of truth, you cannot be objective. Because you don't know what the fuck you're talking about. How can you possibly have an opinion on any given subject that you've got absolutely no knowledge of? The knowledge that I attained informed me that the hard facts of the matter were that people within the prison system didn't have any idea at all of what they were doing with people's lives. All these psychologists and probation officers, the ones who compounded the lie that said I was dangerous and unpredictable, misogynistic and violent, in order to justify the convicted killer syndrome, being in denial and all that, well what did they actually know about my case and conviction?

I appealed against my conviction in 1978, represented myself and lost. I appealed again in 1980, constantly, right the way through the sentence. A separate investigation was started in 1978 led by Superintendent Peter Topping, who eventually got two officers from the Greater Manchester Police convicted. One was Butler, the evil bastard that abused me and concocted my confession. Another officer was acquitted. Topping produced an 837-page document called 'The Topping Report' in 1980 for the CPS. Allegations of bribery and corruption began to surface and by the end of it, Butler was convicted of perverting the course of justice and receiving a bribe. It came to light that there had been a culture of corruption and bribery going on in the force from 1973–79. In March 1983 Butler was sentenced to four years in prison. At my trial the jury were never made aware that Butler was a man capable of corruption and dishonesty in his role as a senior police officer. Had they been aware, their assessment of Butler's so-called evidence may have been considerably different.

The Topping Report' was a damning document against

Greater Manchester Police and amounted to a criminal conspiracy amongst the officers concerned. I mean there was a man who had stabbed someone in the neck during a burglary and paid a bribe to the police to ensure that he was not arrested. Three officers got paid £100 each to advise this man to change his appearance and leave the area. The police then asked the victim who got stabbed to identify a different suspect, who was not the burglar. That was the kind of shit going on in the force on a regular basis.

The Topping Report' came into existence in 1980. Meanwhile my solicitor and I were writing to the Home Office, begging them to reinvestigate and look at the points I was making. In response they suppressed the evidence, year in, year out. All in all, seven Under Secretaries of State wrote to me saying that Butler's corruption had no bearing on my conviction. When I complained about the fact that bloodstained jeans had been submitted to the court as an exhibit, Nicholas Baker wrote back saying, 'I cannot comment at this distance.'

In 1987 I met an investigative journalist called Eammon O'Neil and he started working with my lawyer to help me fight my case. By 1993 we had contacted the Forensic Science Service and discovered that the police had taken it upon themselves to deliberately alter the forensic evidence against Robert Hill in order to eliminate him from their enquiries. None of this had been made available to the court at my trial but still the Home Office refused to refer my case back to the Court of Appeal. I could have been acquitted ten, fifteen years ago but instead the whole system buried the evidence. After completing a documentary with Scottish Television we handed in a petition for an appeal to Michael Howard and hey presto, it was rejected.

The British criminal justice system and successive governments, both Labour and Conservative, have turned lying into an art form. They whip us with a one-sided morality and the British public must now be able to see that the scales of justice are unfairly balanced. Of course not many solicitors will take pro-bono cases on either. There's no money to be made in it. Robert Lizar took my case on pro-bono and he never earned a penny from it for the sixteen years that he represented me. He fought for me for sixteen years for nothing. That's an admirable trait, someone who truly believes in justice. He knew I was innocent because there were just too many holes in my case. It was his gut instinct after reading the case – too many pieces of the jigsaw missing. People on the street could see that my case was a fit-up yet allegedly intelligent, educated people working in the prison system turned their back on me. Why?

So on it went in prison, with prison people playing their allotted roles in society. Shakespeare said, 'The world's a stage and we're all actors.' Well that to me is the fucking problem. Everybody's acting a part because they don't know who the fuck they are themselves. That's what's frightening. The truth is being yourself. Anything else and you are living a fucking lie. So all I could be was innocent and the system was wrong. It was wrong for psychologists to say, 'You need this course, you need that course, you're dangerous, you're unpredictable, you're violent, you're irrational, you're psychotic. You don't remember committing the crime.'

They refused to listen to me proclaiming my innocence and waving my papers. I had to write a letter to my solicitor and take it on a visit saying, 'They're going to try and section me under the Mental Health Act. I don't know where and I don't know when. They're going to try and say, 'Committed the crime and doesn't know he did it.' Well I could never fit that category because I was arrested four months after the crime. I'm supposed to have signed a confession of my own accord and my own free will four months after the murder. So why would I be suffering from a memory blank all of a sudden from then on?

So although they tried to section me because it was convenient for them, they couldn't get away with it. And it's one of those Hollywood myths, when people think that everybody in jail says they're innocent to try and get out. In actual fact it isn't easy to protest your innocence. It's like if you show kindness or love in prison it's taken for a weakness. So you have to be pretty tough to be yourself in the face of a lie for twenty-five years, not only where psychologists are concerned but with the inmates too. All it does for the most part is get you a much longer sentence and far more arbitrary punishment.

I was offered parole ten years ago on condition that I admitted the crime. Well how can I accept anyone calling me a murderer or treating me like one if I'm not a murderer? I had no problem refusing parole because I wanted the truth to endure, not just for me but for Annie Walsh. My ma asked me to take parole too, not to blackmail me emotionally but because she really wanted me out of prison. I wanted my name cleared though. Truth and justice were far more important to me than freedom even though my ma and I were both hurting so badly.

Not only did me and my ma do the sentence, it was the victim's family too. The injustice has been compounded against them. The police told them a pack of manufactured lies from beginning to end. They still haven't contacted the victim's family to speak to them about the investigation. I spoke to Annie Walsh's spirit every night for twenty-five years and asked her to guide me through the experience I was being forced to endure. If she knew that I didn't kill her then I believed she would guide me spiritually – and I believe I have been guided. I want justice for Annie Walsh and her family now. The justice they deserved twenty-five years ago.

In 1983 Dr Dorothy Speed, the head of the psychiatric department inside HMP Long Lartin, made an internal request to the Home Office to investigate my case as a possible miscarriage of justice. In June 1984 she wrote, 'His uncooperative and anti-authority behaviour throughout the 7 years of imprisonment (with a recommendation of 15 years) is in keeping with that of a wrongfully convicted man. I would recommend that his case be reviewed under the terms of 'HO C1 21/84 (Miscarriage of Justice).'

The Home Office replied with their usual apathetic response to Dr Speed in October 1984. 'The case has been carefully considered in the light of all available information but no grounds have been found for any action in respect of Brown's conviction.'

Fifteen years later in 1999–2000 a higher psychologist named Narcie Kelly wrote a report after reading all the documentation (legal papers and prison records) to my case. She correlated a report that expressed grave concern, serious doubts and misgivings about the safety of my conviction. For this psychologist in the prison department, my case had become an ethical issue and a crisis of conscience as she was then told in no uncertain terms by Elizabeth Bird (head of the psychology department) to withdraw the said report and not submit it to the relevant authorities. Narcie Kelly was sacked because she refused to withdraw a report that she saw as the truth, and Elizabeth Bird was rewarded with promotion to Head of the Regional Psychology Unit for all prisons in the Devon area.

How can any department, organisation, institution, group of people or individual regardless of creed, colour, gender or religion, rehabilitate, liberate, educate, love, care and teach people some sense of moral integrity when they emphatically do *not* possess any sense of moral or intellectual integrity? Those who do possess some sense of moral and intellectual integrity, those who are willing to act on their own ethical beliefs and principals, are severely punished and condemned for searching for the truth.

Instead, a distorted truth is used to paint a picture of the system in perfect working order, because appearances have become more important than reality. Psychology is not a science, it is more of an art form, and these artists plagiarise themselves by painting by numbers. They use psychological ploys to illustrate things they simply have no knowledge of, they possess no empirical criterion whatsoever on the situation or circumstances of any individualistic, recidivistic behaviour. It is all theory, theory, theory. No truth. No fact. Just theory. Their theories keep life-sentence prisoners incarcerated for years longer than the tariff or the sentence the judge passes. If psychology departments inside their 'forensic environments' cannot evaluate or assess the guilty in a truthful capacity, how can they assess the innocent? Put simplistically it is all about self-promoting aggrandisement. These psychologists have absolute autonomy, carte blanche to wield their power over the prisoner with theories pertaining to the individual particular crime. Any psychologist will tell you that there is no such thing as the absolute truth, which in itself is an absolutely ridiculous theory. Because empirically the fundamental truths are:

I WAS FALSELY CONVICTED FOR THE MURDER OF ANNIE WALSH. I WAS FALSELY IMPRISONED FOR TWENTY-FIVE YEARS. I AM AN INNOCENT MAN AND I AM NOT, NEVER WAS, NEVER WILL BE RESPONSIBLE FOR THE DEATH OF ANNIE WALSH.

Those are three fundamental truths.

———

Defiant and dignified were the only words I could use to describe Rob Brown, a small Scotsman, as he waited that morning at the CA for the judge to pass judgment upon him yet again. It was no wonder the courtroom felt so restless. Virtually everyone listening to the judge ramble through the horrific factors of the case already knew Rob was innocent and had probably known for years. Letitia Malone, with whom Rob and his girlfriend had lived in 1977, says that Rob had been enthralled by the television series *Rich Man, Poor Man*, which was screened every Friday night. Malone says that she definitely watched the episode with him. It was screened between 10.30 p.m. and 12.15 a.m. on Friday 28 January 1977 – the date and time of Annie Walsh's death.

It was impossible, given all the uncovered truths, that Rob could remain convicted and the prosecution case had all but collapsed. Since the CCRC had started investigating his case five years ago, they had uncovered even more evidence. Linguistic experts agreed that Brown's confession was fabricated. Added to this was the non-disclosure of forensic evidence that implicated Robert Hill and the evidence of police corruption.

It takes a victim of a miscarriage of justice to know how twisted British justice can be though. I quickly picked out the faces of Paddy Hill, Satpal Ram and Raphael Rowe in the courtroom. They had all had to learn what it was like to lose an appeal. In July 2002, Rob had lodged a bail application in the hope that he would be released on humanitarian grounds ahead of his appeal. His frail, seventy-three-year-old mother had not long to live and more than anything in the world Rob wanted to be able to put his arms around her and look after her in the time she had left. His QC had believed that the grounds for his appeal were so strong given the overwhelming dossier of evidence they could present to the court, that a judge would grant bail in such circumstances. It was not to be so. Mr Justice Roderick Evans (the same judge incidentally who, a month earlier, dismissed charges of manslaughter against the five police officers in Christopher Alder's case) had listened to all the evidence and still refused Brown bail.

After just eighteen minutes in the CA that day it was suddenly over. Rob was free at last. I heard Lord Justice Rose mumble, 'We could not possibly be sure on what we have heard that the jury, had they known what we know, would have reached the same verdict. It is, to put it at its lowest, a possibility that they might have reached a quite different verdict.'

A sigh of relief washed over the room and people began to get up. I waited in confusion, glancing all around and back towards Judge Rose, waiting for him to continue. Judge Rose was now silent. Then I frowned, quite disorientated with the whole procedure. Rob was a free man, that much was clear to me. I turned to look back and just caught his back as he disappeared out of the cage but I stayed where I was seated, suddenly burning with a hundred questions as people flocked to the exits. What about the corrupt policemen who'd ruined twenty-five years of his life? What about Rob's previous appeals and petitions that had been ignored? What about the Home Office who had known much of this evidence years ago and simply sat on it, wishing away the constant protestations of innocence that had come from Rob as he languished in his cell, trapped with real-life serial killers, rapists? What about all the forensic evidence that had been suppressed and doctored?

I got up to follow others out of the courtroom into the hallway, wild with contagious delight on one level. A man had cleared his name and been set free. But no one had apologised to Robert Brown. The three law lords, on hearing the evidence, hadn't announced plans to trace Detective Inspector Butler or any of the other officers involved and serve the public by jailing them. They hadn't seemed surprised or disgusted by what they'd just read out. The way the judges got up to leave the room left me icy cold. Didn't they give a damn about Rob, his mum, Annie Walsh or anybody else? I had always believed that justice was the duty of judges and was left shocked by the depth of my mixed feelings. I made a conscious effort not to vomit over the polished wooden pews as I left.

Even so, Robert Brown was about to start the first day of a new life and his mother had lived to see it. They would be reunited, a mother and her son, together at last. Then I thought about Annie Walsh and my heart sank again. She hadn't received a shred of justice but had most likely wept tears in heaven for Rob. Had the real killer claimed more victims over the years?

I followed friends, campaigners and legal figures out of the Royal Courts into the sunshine and turned like many others, to watch Rob meet the onslaught of press. They immediately vied for his attention, pushing cameras and microphones as close to his head as they could. If only the same enthusiasm had pervaded when he'd needed national media support while inside. I noticed Paddy standing beside him, a protective arm thrown casually across a shoulder as the press began firing away.

I've been out six months now and it's quite difficult to grasp the enormity of what I've been through. I mean twenty-five years? I can't even comprehend it now. I'd like to live my life in anonymity but if you're offered a platform then you might as well take it for the benefit of the future generations. All I'm trying to do now is to get a designated independent body to investigate the police. I mean Greater Manchester Police were sanctioned to reinvestigate my case themselves in 1993. That involved a Mr Hunchbach coming to visit me in prison and telling me that if I dropped the allegations I was making against the police, my case would be reopened more quickly. Fucking great.

Home Secretaries must have colluded with the Greater Manchester Police to keep The Topping Report' quiet. The whole report had a Public Interest Immunity certificate slapped on it (PII) (otherwise known as a gagging order) and it was only made available to the court by the CCRC who made a written request to the CPS for any files on Detective Inspector Butler. It was sent a week before my appeal. Greater Manchester Police had a copy of the report, so why didn't they bring it up sooner? Why did The Topping Report' only come to light a week before my appeal? Who disclosed it and why now after twenty years? Even now I've only seen twenty pages of the report. There could well be other victims of miscarriages of justice hidden conveniently in the rest of that report. I've no doubt that there are countless others.

My MP, John Robertson, said that even the Home Secretary of State cannot get access to The Topping Report'. So what, are we living in a fucking police state or something? Who's got The Topping Report' then? I phoned Topping up and spoke to him at home. I thanked him for putting Butler behind bars in 1983 and asked him why he wouldn't talk about the report. He was terrified and wouldn't talk to me. They're hiding something. There has to be a bigger agenda to it.

The doctrine of PII stops evidence from being disclosed and it becomes exempt on 'public interest' grounds. How many unfair trials has legislation like this caused? A demand for secrecy is always based on the higher interests of the state rather than the 'public interest'. The public interest in doing justice to an individual and the need for fairness should far outweigh any other 'public interest'. Surely the public should decide what is in their interests and what, quite plainly here, isn't? PII claims are unnecessary and undesirable in the criminal justice system. Nobody should have the authority to 'judge' what evidence is relevant to the defence. In a criminal trial where the defendant is subject to PII, there can be no doubt that there is a powerful possibility that it has come about through the biased and dishonest opinions expressed by government ministers and the police. They should be open to direct challenge.

How can our government, our criminal justice system and our prison system liberate or rehabilitate if they can't tell the truth even if they wanted to? You cannot liberate anybody without the truth. You cannot have justice as a concept on its own without truth. There is no truth without love. So all these concepts on their own don't stand up but, collectively combined, you get love, truth, respect and justice. We don't treat each other in society with love, truth, respect and justice on a daily basis, either individually or in general. So can we really expect our criminal justice system and our government to give us love, truth, respect and justice when we can't give it to each other? That's what makes me really sad when I see us as one species that can't even get on with each other because of colour or religion. Life is simplistic but humans complicate it with trivia and nonsense. Things that could be solved in a moment are complicated intellectually, by people who haven't got the faintest fucking idea what they're doing. That's what frightens me because I've seen it close up and personal for twenty-five years every day. I saw people at work in the prison system with their hands-on approach. None of it works and they know it. But they make money out of it. They say things like, 'Oh if I can just save one person from being murdered….' Well, yeah, great, but what about all the innocent people inside who are dehumanised for it? One person can be saved but thousands of us rot while the guilty are treated with courses, and 'help'.

Anyone with no self-esteem can get a job with the prison system, go in and look down at all the inmates and get off on it. Their attitude is like, 'Yeah, I'm in a position where I can pretend that I help people and get a title.' These people aren't answerable to anyone and the Home Office just goes on along with it. It's fucking crazy.

Since I came out I've been careful about how I've conducted myself. I don't drink and I'm very careful about who's around me. I don't suffer fools gladly. People thought when I came out that I'd drink heavily, be angry, aggressive and get involved with the wrong type of people. I was angry and aggressive for twenty-five years so to go back there would be extremely foolish of me. Drinking isn't a turn-on and I don't like drunk people around me anyway. If I see people behaving kind of precariously, I'll tell them the next day. The first six weeks that I was out and meeting people, life flashed by me so quickly it was like a kaleidoscope of vision but I've stepped back since then. I can see the bigger picture and I want to keep people distant from me until I've weighed them up.

People have said to me, 'Oh you're not going to survive out there. It's all changed and it's become a violent, drug-cultured, very different world.' Well I find it's the other way round. People are wide open and receptive and it's helped me to adjust. Sometimes I need to be by myself and I'll go off walking around at night because where I live now, it's a nice, quiet area and I'm just across the road from my ma. People told me I'd get panic attacks and have difficulty crossing roads and going on trains. I've asked people not to categorise me. My situation is unique and that makes me unique. To come out like I have done... you can look at other victims of miscarriages of justice and to a certain extent they are broken, damaged people. But believe me when I say that the police could come back to me and fit me up all over again and I would fight the whole system again. They could probably do it as well, what with all the latest scientific bullshit they're trying to advocate to the public. All this DNA 1 in 50,000,000 bullshit. It's all lies and disinformation.

By the time I'd educated myself, moving around the prison system the majority of the people I met and spoke to on a daily basis (and no disrespect to any prisoners) were young, uneducated recidivists. The reasons are obvious to me – lack of interest at school, lack of family structure, etc. I mean your average petty criminal isn't taught at school to love your brother and sister whatever colour, class or creed; embrace each other and treat each other with love and warmth and humanity. The schools don't do that. The schools in Scotland are still segregated because of sectarianism: Catholics go to their schools and Protestants go to theirs. There's a minority of mixed schools but not many. Now why is that in the twenty-first century? Why not integrate all religions: Muslims, Jews, Protestants, Catholics, Sikhs, everybody. Why not let everybody learn about each other's culture and let everybody become friends, from juniors and right up? That's the only way to break today's barriers. Nationalism in itself is a false fucking emotion that means nothing. It's founded on nothing except brainwashing with a flag and it's a big part of why everyone's at each other's throats today. So I come out of jail in 2002 and there's the fucking BNP in Burnley for fuck sake. What kind of world are we living in?

I went back to prison after I got out and shook certain screws' hands outside HMP Wymot and I thanked certain screws for treating me like a human being during the last twelve months of my sentence. It's the first time I'd ever been treated like a human being and it blew me away. At first I'd thought they were trying to lull me into a false sense of security, but they weren't. It wasn't many screws, only the block staff and a couple of screws from the wing. It got to the stage when I was in the punishment block where they'd actually unlock my door – never been done before – and let me go and get a cup of tea. I could walk about the block and they'd let me use the phone. They were giving me things that you never used to get given in punishment blocks. I even had a governor who used to bring me in books to read and a couple of the screws even said, 'Look, we know you're innocent but we're scared to say it, mate. We've read all your letters, paperwork and your newspaper cuttings.'

I refuse to become a victim now that I am out. I don't need someone like Dr Adrian Grounds or any other psychologist out there to say, 'Oh, this guy's dysfunctional and he can't go to pubs and he can't do this or that.' Yes, I know prison damages people. I've seen people become vacant one night and never come back. I've seen plenty of other people hang themselves. But that's not me. I could be a raving lunatic if I wanted to but the point is, I'm not. I never became institutionalised. I did things for myself, with my own beliefs and thought for myself. I had my own philosophies and code of values and I certainly didn't follow the system.

I'll be the first to admit that I went down the route of taking drugs when I couldn't handle the pain any longer. I probably can't convey this with words when I say 'pain' but I'm really talking about every little thing in life that people take for granted every day. Seeing my mother and being able to put my arms around her and take care of her. Seeing children grow up and hearing laughter. Seeing beauty, feeling warmth and kindness and living in the elements – rain, snow, sunshine and blue sky, the smell of flowers.

By 1990 I was fucking bewildered and so cut up and lost in the pain. That was when the whole prison system exploded with heroin. Imagine the size of one jail, right? It typically has six wings and houses nearly 600 men. How much heroin would you need to keep 400–500 of those prisoners going, week in and week out? It couldn't come in via visits, could it, unless every prisoner was getting a visit every day? It's like you could get into debt for speed, weed or valium. But once you got into debt for heroin, people would stick knives into you and throw boiling cooking fat over you. The violence was crazy and the screws encouraged it because then they could control the prisoners. Heroin destroyed any semblance of prisoner solidarity. I know it was detrimental to me in the long term. It emaciated, weakened and almost destroyed my will to live.

If I could pass on any of my experience to people who are behind bars today, guilty or innocent, I would advise them to follow the path of truth, love and righteous peace, to not be scared of doing so, and to also stay well away from heroin. All you have to be is yourself, you don't have to follow patriarchal or nationalistic roles. I also recommend a book called *The Prophet* by Kahlil Gibran, to anyone inside or outside of prison. It's only about forty pages long and one of the easiest books to read. If people read one page of that book every day they'd be far more enlightened and rehabilitated than anyone caught in the clutches of prison could ever be.

So the degradation and the deprivation that I endured made me the man I am today. I think that out of everything bad there has to come some good, if you want it to, but you have to nurture and cultivate the good and that's what I did. I didn't come out of prison just to take more drugs, get drunk and sleep around. There are things I want to do. I want to help people that are less fortunate than myself. I've been warned that I could suffer from depression and anxiety and I know that I have to keep off the drugs. You can characterise and stereotype people but I know I'm a level-headed individual and I've got my feet firmly planted on the ground. But I'm not putting myself on any kind of moral pedestal and if I confront problems in the future then I will pick up the phone and ask the right people for advice.

I'm not bitter either. I'm capable of taking a look around the world and living in the knowledge that there are people much worse off than me. Handicapped children, blind people, people living in abject poverty in Africa and I have to put things into perspective. We all know that every system is flawed and we could never have a perfect system but we have to try and make it better. I'm not the nineteen-year-old boy who went into prison. Once you walk out that gate you have to be the man that you are.

The reservoirs of strength that I've got have been given as a gift and I'm determined not to throw it away. Now is the time for the system to try and put right what went wrong in 1977. If they can't do that for people like me and Annie Walsh, the whole British public have got no chance of ever getting justice from the criminal justice system. I have been raped of twenty-five years of my life. I have been raped spiritually, emotionally, mentally and physically, while those who uphold the criminal justice system held me down and watched me slowly being destroyed, vilified and dehumanised on a daily basis. Anybody who takes away the life of another human being for twenty-five years has got to be guilty of committing one of the worst crimes of the century. Those people are collectively guilty of compounding the lies, the pain, the suffering and injustice that I endured for twenty-five years of my life. You all know who you are.

I would like to thank my mother, who also served twenty-five years of a life sentence, who also endured the lie, the pain, the suffering and injustice, who showed remarkable strength and love as only a mother can. I would also like to give my undying gratitude to Robert Lizar who did not receive a single penny for the hard work and endeavour in his fight to free me from captivity. I would like to thank Eamonn O'Neil who played a major role in my release as an investigative journalist. It was refreshing and enlightening for me as a man who had been held hostage by the British judicial system to find a journalist with a deep-rooted sense of moral integrity.

I would like also to thank Paddy Hill of the Birmingham Six who in many, many ways has been an inspiration and a tower of strength for all miscarriages of justice since his release in 1991. I would also like to thank John McManus and MOJO, as well as the Alabama Three, for the phenomenal support and loyalty and friendship they have shown to me, and to other miscarriages of justice. I would also like to thank the British public for the overwhelming support that they have given to me since my release.

'Those who are paid to represent the criminal justice system and the prison system are not pedagogue extraordinaires, nor are they prophets of wisdom or walking constitutions of knowledge on anyone's life.'

Robert Brown

Satpal Ram

Nick Cohen once wrote,

> Unless you've been through a miscarriage of
> justice campaign, you can't know how hard it is
> to take the smallest of steps.

I did not understand how literally this statement had been written until I first came across the case of Satpal Ram and met some of the people who had supported him in his own fight for justice.

Joining a struggle in a bid to help secure someone's freedom is no easy commitment, as experience has since shown me. To have an already overfilled life of your own and to choose to commit a part of it, however small, to someone residing in a maximum-security prison, is not for the faint- or cold-hearted. The people that supported Satpal are all first and foremost people who refused to accept the message of racial inferiority that his case and history assumed. By the time I became involved (by which time Satpal had already served twelve years of a ten-year tariff) they included a core group of campaigners, with an ever-widening network of support coming from people from all walks of life. The more I looked into his case, visiting, listening to what he had to say, studying the masses of paperwork that covered his case history, and talking to his family, friends and lawyers, the more effort I found myself making on his behalf and the more infuriated and powerless I began to feel as the weeks of my involvement turned into months and then years.

For a start you have the prisoner to worry about. Will campaign efforts, for instance to have the truth told in the public domain, cause more harm than good to the prisoner who is caged behind a wall of secrecy at the mercy of often violent officers? The more the prisoner resists the system, the more brutality he or she may face. Yet when asked this question during the calls Satpal made to friends and family, he'd always reply,

> Things can't get any worse. The system is riddled with racism and too many people have suffered years of torture as a result. Why shouldn't I speak out about it?

He'd speak with the utmost certainty and I chose to live with the belief that if campaigners could keep his case in the public eye, it might afford him some protection. It was also felt crucial that the public learn the details of his case and protest, ironically perhaps, in the name of justice.

For Satpal, phone calls pretty much formed his only contact with the outside world. During the last two years of imprisonment he received regular visits, but prior to that was often left in the isolation block, on a diet of a meagre sandwich a day, for months at a time. It was not uncommon for him to be transferred with no notice to a prison 200 miles away from his family and over the sixteen years of his imprisonment Satpal was transferred to over seventy-four different prisons, having been moved every few weeks.

Racists ruined Satpal's life when he was nineteen years old. On the evening of 16 November 1986, he'd decided to go to a local Bangladeshi restaurant to eat, accompanied by two friends. They lived in Handsworth, an inner-city area of Birmingham troubled by dilapidated housing, racial discrimination, unemployment and poverty. The community felt further repressed by heavy-handed policing tactics. Made up of Asian, black and poor white people, Handsworth had been the scene of violent riots throughout 1985. Satpal writes about the incident that led to his imprisonment.

Not long after we ordered our meal and it was while we were waiting for our meal to arrive, we noticed a group of six people enter the restaurant and sit down to the left of our table. They were shouting and swearing and the language they were using was racially offensive and derogatory. We tried to ignore it but it was difficult because of the racist nature of the remarks they were making. The waiter arrived with our meal. While he was serving it, I commented that I liked the background music that was playing and asked if he wouldn't mind turning up the volume slightly.

As soon as I asked the question, a man who was with the group of six stood up angrily from his table and said he didn't want any Paki-Wog music on. He became further enraged when I simply replied that I hadn't been talking to him and he picked up a wine glass. He broke it on the table and came darting towards me, stabbing me in the face with the glass. I started to bleed heavily. At the same time his friends also got up and started shouting obscenities, encouraging him to attack me again. They even threw plates and glasses at me though they must have seen me bleeding. Of course I was scared. There were six of them and I was with two of my friends, a white girl called

Evelyn and an Asian male, Navinder. Physically, this man was much bigger than me and I was in fear for my life.

I managed to push the man (who I later learnt was Clarke Pearce) away after he stabbed me on the first occasion. He stepped back a little but moved towards me again. He aimed the glass at my face and then stabbed me in my arm. At this point his intentions were clear and I was certain that in his state of mind, he wouldn't stop until he'd maimed or killed me. I didn't know what to do and couldn't run because I had my back to the restaurant wall. I worked in a warehouse cutting the bands off hessian boxes and used a small works knife in my everyday work. The knife was in my pocket at the time and I got it out in an attempt to warn him away. I thought I could stop the attack by scaring him but he still came at me with the glass.

I never intended to kill this man – I'd never seen him before and had no grievance with him. But I was given no choice but to defend myself. Although I was gushing with blood he rushed me again. In the course of defending myself the knife went into him. It was a mess, the tables had been tipped up, I was in complete shock and there were smashed glasses and plates everywhere. Clarke staggered. I remember seeing his eyes filled with hatred and although he was injured he tried to reach me again but fell down. His friends were still shouting things like, 'Fucking black bastard' at me.

I stood there in shock until Evelyn led me to the toilets. She took the knife from me and placed it on the towel machine. I knew I needed to go to the hospital urgently as the bleeding wouldn't stop. We walked out and dropped Evelyn at her house while Navinder accompanied me to Sandwell General Hospital in West Bromwich. I received medical attention for my wounds and then we caught a taxi back to Handsworth. Navinder went home and I went on to another friend's house for the night. The gash in my cheek had needed stitches and I didn't want my parents to see how I'd been hurt.

It wasn't until the following day that I realised Clarke had died. I first heard it on the radio and just could not believe it. Much later I learnt that he'd been uncooperative and abusive to a doctor trying to treat him. He'd pulled out a drip and gone into shock. I was confused because when I'd left the restaurant he'd still been swearing at me, very much alive, even though he'd been injured. I didn't know what to do and ended up staying with friends, not leaving the house. I tried to convince myself that it never happened but after a few days realised I couldn't stay there forever.

As time passed I went back to Handsworth and friends told me that the police had raided their houses looking for me. Everywhere I went I heard the same story. I had to see my parents as I knew they'd be worried sick. I needed to reassure them that I was okay and tell them what had happened. I phoned an uncle's house and asked that my parents meet me there. When me met and I'd explained everything, my dad told me that the police were making his life hell, coming to the house at all hours of the day and harassing both him and my mother. It was at this point that I decided to voluntarily give myself up to the police.

My uncle contacted a solicitor, John Morgan, who collected me and took me to his office. I told him everything that had happened and he told me not to worry, agreeing that it was a clear case of self-defence. He advised me to tell the police everything and I agreed. I got taken to Steelhouse Lane Police Station and effectively surrendered myself eight days after the incident took place.

I was placed into a cell for almost two hours waiting to be interviewed. They asked me questions during this time but I refrained from responding until my solicitor was present. I was told that the post mortem had revealed a 'number' of stab wounds to the deceased. I was sure there could only have been one wound but they were making out like I must have made some kind of frenzied attack.

I told them, 'It happened so quickly, I was in a state of confusion. I can't explain the other stab wounds.' I couldn't. None of it made any sense.

The police then made out like I'd attacked Pearce with the knife and suggested that I'd used a glass too. They were saying things like, 'Those were deliberate acts by you to cause him really serious injury. He didn't just fall against your knife.'

I replied, 'That's a lie. I did not want to kill him. I'm sorry he died.'

I only had the knife on me in the first place because I'd been in a rush to go out straight after work and forgot about it.

About half an hour after my solicitor left they charged me with murder. I couldn't believe it in one sense. I was only twenty when it happened and terrified to have been put in the whole situation. But on the other hand, it had taken me eight days to pluck up the courage to tell the truth in the first place. I wasn't stupid. They were white and I'm Asian. There was open hostility towards most Asians in the area at the time. The National Front had deliberately targeted the area and were allowed, by the police, to hold meetings in Handsworth, where they deliberately incited racial hatred and openly advocated attacks on black and Asian people. There was always the fear of attack. That there were six of them didn't matter to the police. That there were both Asian and white witnesses didn't matter either.

I spent the night in a cell and Morgan came to see me briefly in the morning. When I told him about the charge he told me not to worry, saying that it would be dropped at a later date. I actually trusted him! Then I was taken to the court.

Once there I was immediately confronted by a lynch mob who were hell-bent on hurling racist remarks at me like, 'Fucking paki.' I was spat on and physically attacked. About a dozen prison officers had to surround me for my protection from Clarke's family and friends. Then I got remanded in custody. I didn't know whether I was coming or going. I had not come to terms with my imprisonment and my mind was in turmoil.

Satpal was kept in custody from 24 November 1986; he turned twenty years old in January and stayed in custody until the day of the trial on 5 June 1987. His mind was obviously one of great confusion and vulnerability.

The social and psychological costs to Satpal of being remanded were substantial. From a legal perspective alone, research has shown that defendants remanded in custody are far more likely to be found guilty, perhaps because of the effect of being seen in the dock rather than in front of the bench. The presence of a racially hostile, spitting, white crowd would have further debased his chances of a fair hearing. With no access to competent legal advice, mounting an effective defence was fraught with difficulty.

In their brief to counsel the solicitors put Satpal's case clearly as self-defence, which is no crime at all. Leading counsel Douglas Draycott, QC, advised that,

> In an effort to defend himself after being attacked with the glass, he struck the deceased. Clearly the defendant will argue that he was defending himself.

Then on 1 June 1987, just a few days before the trial began, the solicitors visited Satpal and held a forty-minute conference with him. During that time they advised Satpal to change his legal defence completely. Satpal had always maintained that he had acted in self-defence but his solicitors advised him to change his plea to provocation, a defence that simply reduces murder to manslaughter. The essence of this defence is that a person loses self-control due to the words or behaviour of another and kills deliberately under the effect of this loss of self-control. Satpal never said that he had lost his self-control nor did he ever say that he had killed deliberately.

In Satpal's words,

> Draycott talked me into pleading provocation. I remember him saying that he could not put forward self-defence because of the number of wounds found on the deceased. I didn't really argue with him because I thought he was acting in my interests. I left the conducting of my defence to him, which was the worst mistake of my life. They also insisted that I shouldn't give evidence in my own defence. I was upset by this because I wanted to tell my side of the story, but after a while I again went along with what they said because, again, I thought they were acting in my best interests. I had no knowledge of the law.

Had Draycott properly examined the pathologist's evidence, he would have concluded that the actual number of knife wounds amounted to two. The remaining wounds were superficial and caused by glass – not by a frenzied knife attack as had originally been made out. One knife wound was in the deceased's back but this is not inconsistent with self-defence if the attacker was standing close to Satpal, sideways on.

During the trial, witnesses were called to give evidence in Satpal's defence. This consisted of his two friends, and two Bengali-speaking waiters from the Sylhet district of Bangladesh, whose ability to speak the English language was limited to the general ordering of meals at the restaurant. There were three other Asian witnesses who had been eating but they left the restaurant immediately after the incident and were not traced.

Despite an obvious language barrier, no interpreter was provided for the Bengali-speaking witnesses and the judge, Justice Ognall, advised that he himself would act as interpreter, though he did not speak a word of Bengali. Another waiter who witnessed the incident, a student who spoke English fluently, was not called to give evidence. These witnesses were crucial to Satpal's defence and the failure to provide an interpreter effectively muted those who did appear.

Satpal had no opportunity to put his explanation of self-defence to the jury and the judge asked the jury to consider a verdict of murder as opposed to provocation, stating that he had been acting in his 'right mind' when Clarke Pearce received the knife wounds. At no time did the judge place the incident in its true context, which was that Satpal had been acting in self-defence during a racist attack, which had been initiated by Clarke Pearce. In his summing up, the judge told the jury to disregard Navinder's statement to the police, as he had been charged as a co-accused until dismissed from the case at an early stage. He advised that Evelyn's evidence should be looked at 'with a special caution', because she had helped Satpal 'via the back streets to avoid detection'.

The trial lasted just three days and the jury returned with a verdict of guilty. Justice Ognall sentenced Satpal to life imprisonment, with a recommended tariff of ten years.

Devastated by the verdict against him, Satpal was dealt further blows by the legal system in that twice he was knocked back on appeal. Appeal Court Justice Lord Lane advised that it was not the function of the court to review the advocacy of trial counsel and that mistakes committed by defending counsel did not constitute grounds for appeal. Satpal, however, remained determined to fight his conviction. As the years in prison took their toll, he always maintained that the lawyers he was provided with failed to present his case properly to the court. In failing to do so, the jury were never advised to decide on the real issue – whether Satpal acted in self-defence as supported by independent witnesses, or whether Clarke's family were right and that Clarke was the innocent victim of a ruthless murderer.

With no legal avenues left to which he could turn, Satpal focussed on others inside who he felt had been wrongfully convicted, including the Birmingham Six, Guildford Four, Winston Silcott and the M25 Three. He campaigned for decent prison conditions and protested via his campaign and supporters, at the daily brutality and squalor that prisoners faced. By virtue of challenging his case, he attempted to bring a more progressive law into communities and an antiracist agenda was key to his concept of justice, as was ending other forms of subordination.

I wondered whether Satpal was the sort of person willing to pay with his life if necessary, for progressive change in the legal and penal framework. On one occasion he was summoned for a routine cell search where five officers searched his cell and then ordered him to strip for a body search. In accordance with prison rules, he requested some privacy, asking that the door to his cell be closed for the search. They responded by subjecting him to a brutal assault.

> I was grabbed by one of the officers and thrown to the floor. The other officers joined in the attack. My thumbs were bent backwards and my arms were twisted and forced behind my back. Somebody grabbed me by the hair and forcefully pulled my head backwards. They then proceeded to rain blows to my body.

The officers fastened a pair of ratchet handcuffs to his wrists, tightening them until they cut through his skin. He was then dragged down a corridor to the segregation unit where he was forcibly stripped and repeatedly beaten again.

A doctor came down to see Satpal afterwards but refused to take photographic evidence of his injuries. When visited later in the day by the Board of Visitors and the governor, they also refused his request to allow him a call to his solicitor. Satpal started a hunger strike.

> I spent all day without food and water and then a long night in the box having to endure total

deprivation. I had to sleep on the floor in freezing conditions and didn't have access to a bed, toilet or a sink.

He would insist,

> Do not think my case is an isolated one. Many other prisoners have been subjected to similar treatment up and down the country. We are subjected to psychological abuse, intimidation, deprivation and brutality is a daily occurrence.

This level of abuse was to continue and when added up over sixteen years, Satpal spent over six years in isolation units.

In November 1997 he wrote the following statement from HMP Nottingham, following a parole review:

> On December 12 1997, the Parole Board are due to consider my case for possible release under the terms of the Life Licence. I have now served over eleven years in prison for defending myself against a racially motivated attack. Since my conviction I have consistently maintained that I acted in self-defence and that I was the victim of a totally unprovoked attack. Up until now I have been denied any form of redress by the appeals process. My last appeal was rejected in November 1995.

> When you consider that all the evidence against me supports my claim of self-defence, my

continued imprisonment can only be called unjustifiable. I feel that I should now be released from prison. After my trial in June 1987 the then Chief Justice Lord Lane made a recommendation that I should serve ten years in prison. This tariff date expired in November last year. I have now started my twelfth in prison. The Home Office has upped my tariff date and this clearly amounts to political interference. I have served the sentence imposed upon me by the courts, now I am being made to serve an additional sentence for political whims.

On 6 January 1998, the Parole and Lifer Group asked the Governor of HMP Nottingham to inform Satpal of the following:

The Secretary of State has referred your case to the Parole Board which has not recommended your release for the following reasons:

'Although Mr Ram accepts that he caused the death of his victim, he maintains that his actions did not amount to murder. His behaviour while in custody has been unsatisfactory. He states that he is not a violent man but reports indicate that there have been repeated episodes of violence and other unacceptable behaviour. He has not undertaken any offence-related work.

'Mr Ram should be aware that the Parole Board is required to proceed on the assumption that prisoners have committed those offences of which they have been convicted or to which they have pleaded guilty. In the light of Mr Ram's behaviour while in custody and his failure to undertake offence-related work, which may in part be due to his repeated moves between prisons at short intervals of time, the panel felt unable to conclude that the risk of further violence has been reduced to a level at which it could recommend his release or transfer to open conditions. Nevertheless the panel was concerned about the way in which Mr Ram has been and is being moved between prisons and considered it important that he is permitted to stay at one prison for a significant period of time to enable him to settle and for appropriate offence related work to be undertaken.

'The panel recommend that Mr Ram's next parole review should begin in two years' time.'

———————

I would never pretend to understand what it was really like for Satpal, however campaigners made efforts not to receive his phone calls or visit him in total ignorance either. As time went by, I learnt that for all the high talk that would take place on his behalf at the House of Commons and Home Office, nothing seemed to change for the human being buried deep behind it all. There was an incredible degree of vocalising in all the right places and for campaigners timing was an important element of strategic thinking. How much could we hope to attain within a month? When was the best time to defy openly the legal process? When should we sit and wait? For Satpal of course, timing was very different and we tried to balance the process of campaigning with the process of visiting and talking to him.

I intensely dislike prisons. There was an occasion when prison officers coldly insisted that my partner and I visit Satpal behind glass windows in a secure room or not at all. I was treated as though they must have thought I had a stash of drugs to offer him, though searches were routine procedure before any visitor got past the reception anyway.

On another occasion we would be kept waiting for almost an hour in the reception (as other visitors passed through) before being let through for the remaining hour. There was a visit to HMP Blakenhurst, during which, barely twenty minutes into the visit we were abruptly interrupted by a female officer who suddenly snapped without warning at Satpal, making me jump unexpectedly. She looked like she'd walked straight out of *Prisoner Cell Block H*. Satpal was told he had ten minutes remaining before our visit was over. She glared at my partner and me with utter contempt before flexing large biceps and trotting away. Watching her, I was anxious to learn whether other prisoners were treated with such derision but it seemed nobody else was that day. According to my watch we had well over an hour left in visiting time and the room was still bustling with the subdued chatter of other visitors and prisoners.

Satpal advised us to ignore her. I felt claustrophobic as I remembered how many doors I had yet to pass through before I would be free of the repressive stench that pervaded that place. I could no longer relax knowing that she would be coming back and felt almost guilty in the knowledge that we could so easily walk away when Satpal could not.

We sang songs through the rest of that visit. They say where words fail, music speaks and that's how we got through the rest of that visit. We weren't loud or brash – far from it. We simply blocked the rest of the room out and sang, one song after another.

When the prison officer returned about half an hour later to throw the remains of a visiting order at Satpal, my partner had had enough. Outraged, he wasted no time pulling the officer up for her behaviour, his verbal assault making a complete mockery of her authority. It culminated in us being banned from the prison for a month, but was every bit worth it as Satpal was shortly after transferred to an open prison.

After endless months of campaigning it was as if we were working towards some kind of abstract future that we were making up in our minds. We may have been running around, protesting to the government, ministers, lords, the media, just about anyone who would listen in fact (while also taking care of our own immediate needs like employment, housing, family, etc.) but for all our efforts, Satpal was in comparison dancing with the devil. He became increasingly gaunt, underweight and dishevelled after each alleged physical assault, legal knock-back and arbitrary punishment spent in the segregation block.

Abstraction and detachment are great ways to avoid the reality and sheer ugliness of oppression. It is hard to retain contact with someone on a regular basis over the space of years and keep learning about brutality, the latest cruelty, and to know of a life that is mostly stark nothingness, thirst, starvation, humiliation, loneliness, frustration and despair. You have to make a deliberate choice to see points of view from the standpoint of the oppressed. Detachment is great as I say, because it enables us to discuss comfortably issues like justice and freedom, without giving a second's thought to what the concepts mean in real people's lives. The reality and detail of oppression are a crucial starting point before one can spout away about law and theory and strategy. Campaigning was never going to be easy but then that's not why any of us chose to do it. We all came from different backgrounds too and to challenge our assumptions and built-in expectations of one another was sometimes painful, but an important part of maintaining the process.

In 1998, Satpal wrote the following from HMP Frankland:

> Racism within the criminal justice system has been instrumental in criminalising a disproportionate number of black people who are in prison today. Black people constitute seven per cent of the population at large, as opposed to eighteen per cent of the prison population. This reflects the level of bias that exists within the system. Evidence of further discrimination can be found by analysing the official statistics for stop-and-searches carried out in the capital in the year 1994/1995. Out of the 189,000 searches conducted by the Metropolitan Police, 120,000 of them were young black people (Lee Jasper, 1996). This in itself suggests a concerted

systematic attempt at criminalising black people, solely on the basis of preconceived prejudices that target specific sections of the community. Race not only determines who the police arrest, but it is also a decisive factor that influences the way in which the courts view and treat black defendants. For many black people the reality is that when the courts process them, they are more likely to be refused bail and remanded in custody. Black defendants face longer sentences and are also inclined to be the victims of discrimination during the trial phase. In a majority of cases juries are from predominantly all-white, middle-class backgrounds and this can affect the outcome of a trial before the evidence has been heard.

On examining the root causes of miscarriages of justice, a more prominent factor that has led to many wrongful convictions is the role played by the media. Adverse publicity before a trial, or inferences implying a person's guilt has affected the outcome of many trials. Juries are often influenced by what they read in the press and this can prejudice a defendant's chances of a fair hearing. In effect the scales are tipped in favour of the prosecution from a very early stage in any investigation. This imbalance has been reinforced by the fact that the majority of people who come into contact with the criminal justice system are from socially deprived backgrounds in the first instance. Many of those who appear before the courts end up in prison due to a combination of factors, i.e. poverty, debt, unemployment, lack of education and other social conditions which have been frequently ignored by society at large. In essence, as the gap between rich and poor becomes more visible, politicians on both sides of the political divide have been guilty of socially engineering the criminalisation of poor communities throughout the land.

Whether the justice system continues to attain this level of attention depends entirely on its ability to implement fundamental change. At present the judicial process has been seriously undermined by the lack of accountability enjoyed by those in positions of authority. Ultimately it's going to take determined measures to restore its reputation.

———————

In terms of increasing public support and awareness of his case, a significant breakthrough for Satpal occurred in 1998 when the band Asian Dub Foundation were informed about his situation and released a track called 'Free Satpal Ram'. During interviews with the media and the leafleting of venues played in around the world, they were able to create a platform from which people could learn about his case, publicly demand his release and call for a public enquiry into his treatment. Through this medium, other musicians came to learn of his predicament, including Primal Scream and Chumbawumba.

Campaigners used the increased level of public support to capture names and addresses around the world, encouraging all and sundry to channel letters of protest to the Parole Board and the Home Office. If nothing else we became a pain and an embarrassment to the government that refused to be brushed away.

In 1999, civil-rights lawyer Gareth Pierce agreed to take on Satpal's case, appalled by the circumstances of his continued incarceration. She would firmly reiterate,

> There is no good reason for him being imprisoned. A significant number of wrongfully convicted individuals have been marked out by the prison service in the same way as Satpal Ram, as troublemakers in permanent confrontation with the prison system.

Among many other cases, she had worked with Paul Hill and Gerry Conlon of the Guildford Four and Paddy Hill. As far as Pierce was concerned, Satpal was to represent the test anti-racist case, following the botched case of Stephen Lawrence, and the opportunity by which the government could demonstrate a commitment to anti-racism.

When first locked up Satpal had no interest in reading. He then started educating himself and before long, had read books by Nelson Mandela, George Jackson and Mumia Abu Jamal. Their own political struggles and time spent incarcerated in jail represented his own experiences and from these kinds of books he was able to draw strength. Once he'd read law books he began to assert his rights through the application of his ever-increasing knowledge. He went so far as to file a civil suit against prison officers who had assaulted him. Asking him how the hell he managed to stay so positive, he would sing his reply, quoting the IRA hunger striker Bobby Sands:

It lights the dark of the prison cell
It thunders forth its might
It is the undauntable thought my friend
That thought that says I'm right

Organising a one-off demonstration is never easy but to try and sustain a number of demonstrations over an indefinite time frame takes sheer determination. Heavy rain can cut attendance to a handful of supporters, which is also demoralising. I will therefore always remember with a particular feeling of triumph over adversity, turning up with a handful of supporters for a demonstration outside the Parole Board – during a thunderstorm. How effective could that possibly be? There was nobody to hand out leaflets to and nobody to read our hastily-put-together placards. We were getting rapidly soaked.

Then by a stroke of that marvellous thing we call coincidence, the fire alarm went off in Abell House (the building that houses the Parole Board together with several other companies) and before we knew it, about a hundred people had temporarily trooped outside. Placards and leaflets were read with immediate interest. In these sorts of conditions campaigners must have come across as either mad or desperate but our bedraggled presence had workers actually asking questions about why, and how and when. They were stuck with us waiting to go back inside, and most agreed to pass by the Parole Board staff with a leaflet and enquire as to how and why Satpal had been turned down for parole in 1998, and on what basis he would be turned down again. This was now 2000 and Satpal was due another parole hearing. The following photocopied supporting statement from professional psychotherapeutic counsellor Ben Homfray, dated 14 October 1999, was handed out:

Dear Parole and Lifer Group,

I have worked intensely with many ex-offenders who have had violent pasts. I am experienced at making risk-assessments of the people I work with. It would only be honest to say that I have been a long-standing supporter of Satpal's fight to get his case recognised as the miscarriage of justice that it is.

I have known Satpal for the past seven years. We have communicated through letters, phone calls and numerous prison visits. He is a balanced and stable man who knows exactly what he is doing and takes full responsibility for what he has done. In this respect Satpal has always been sorry about the unfortunate death of his assailant back in November 1986 but clearly at great personal cost to himself he has always maintained his actions were in self-defence.

Satpal Ram is undoubtedly angry about his original conviction and the subsequent mistreatment he has frequently incurred in the hands of the prison system. Can you imagine how you would feel if you were wrongly accused of something you didn't do? Then imagine spending thirteen years being punished for this by being denied the most basic freedoms. Of course you would be angry, of course you wouldn't want to accept degrading and humiliating punishment for something you didn't do, and of course you would do what you could to end the mistreatment and prove your innocence.

It is a remarkable testament to the strength of character of Satpal that he has remained so mentally healthy. He shows he is aware of his own feelings and thoughts and is clearly able to articulate them. He is also aware of and responsive to the feelings of others. He is independently minded but does respect and listen to others' opinions. He has an affable and easy-going nature. He is able to form strong and long-lasting friendships with his colleagues, family and supporters, despite having been moved fifty-nine times since his imprisonment. He is an intelligent man who keeps up to date with what's happening on the other side of the prison walls. All these factors collectively point to him being a balanced and fully functioning person.

I strongly believe that were Satpal to be released tomorrow he would be of no significant risk to the public.

Yours sincerely,

Mr B. C. Homfray

Demonstrations continued throughout Satpal's next

parole review. Asian Dub Foundation must have flown around the world twice over singing about Satpal's case, while Primal Scream had released their latest album, *Exterminator*, with a separate information sheet inside the cover of the CD. On one occasion Bobby Gillespie, the lead vocalist of Primal Scream, arranged to visit Satpal in Hull. When Satpal sent him a visiting order he booked the visit but on arriving at the prison, having travelled up from London, prison officers refused to permit him.

Gillespie chuckled as he recalled the incident.

> Satpal told the prison officers that we were high-profile, crazy rock 'n' roll people, and if we weren't let in, we'd get a power generator and a lorry and have a huge gig outside the prison gates! So they let us in. They turn people away all the time. That and the beatings, that's all designed to break him down.

There were over 2,000 separate web pages on the internet calling for his release and it was exhausting to retain contact with the press about one person for so long and still know that for all of it, Satpal remained firmly behind bars. Many protests were directed at the Parole Board but by mid-2000, few people believed that Satpal would be recommended for release. There was absolutely nothing to indicate that he would not go on to spend the next five or ten years in prison, as many had done before him.

In October 2000 the Parole Board finally announced that they would be giving their decision on Satpal's eligibility for parole. The month passed and having still heard nothing, petitions were delivered to Downing Street in person, alongside MPs, lawyers and civil-rights campaigners. Supporters by this time included Imran Khan, the solicitor of the family of Stephen Lawrence; Mohinder and Ramesh Ram, Satpal's brother and nephew; Suresh Grover, co-founder of the National Civil Rights Movement and John McDonnell, MP. The musician Apache Indian had written a reggae track called 'Free Up Satpal Ram' that was shown by *Channel 4 News*, and he brought a coach-load of supporters down from Birmingham.

In May 2001 we learnt that the Parole Board actually *did* make a recommendation but the Home Office had suppressed it for seven months. It had been an unprecedented recommendation supporting Satpal's immediate release. The panel had even said,

> ...the high level of support which is available to Mr Ram in the community will be sufficient to ensure that his rehabilitation from a long sentence of imprisonment can proceed without risk of re-offending. In these exceptional circumstances the panel recommends that he be released on licence without the need for a period in open conditions.

Jack Straw decided that Satpal should spend even longer in prison. Overriding the authority of the Parole Board he rejected the recommendation. Satpal seemed caught in a never-ending quagmire. His mother had just been diagnosed with leukaemia and had not long left to live.

He'd already lost his father while inside. Psychologically, he was taking another battering.

I was dismayed that a politician felt able to extend Satpal's sentence in this way and it seemed to make a mockery of the whole court process. Jack Straw had never so much as met Satpal and certainly had no idea what he was like as a person. It seemed preposterous under the circumstances, a decision that served political purposes rather than any beneficial social purposes. Sentencing takes place during a trial and under Article 6 of the Human Rights Convention a defendant has the right to a fair trial by an independent and impartial tribunal. What right had a politician to interfere?

Then in a landmark decision in May 2002, the European Court of Human Rights ruled that the former Home Secretary Jack Straw had breached the rights of convict Dennis Stafford by keeping him in jail longer than recommended by the Parole Board. The court ruled that a judicial body should make the final decision concerning a prisoner's release, not a politician. Threatened with legal action that continued imprisonment of Satpal was unlawful, the Treasury Solicitor for the Home Office finally agreed to have him released. Satpal walked free on Tuesday 18 June 2002.

Although finally out of prison, Satpal's conviction has not been quashed. The CCRC had been privy to details of his case since 1998 and his lawyers had made lengthy submissions to them that included new witness evidence. A former police superintendent who worked in Handsworth during the riots had described in detail the level of fear and racism experienced and provoked at the time by the National Front. A Bengali-speaking waiter who was not called at the trial had added a submission, covering the explicit racism experienced in the court and the fact that they were spat on and laughed at. Other waiters made representations about how they were misinterpreted and then laughed out of court, and submissions were made concerning the deficiencies of Satpal's original defence.

Unfortunately the above made not an iota of difference to the CCRC, who provisionally rejected Satpal's case. I'd brought up the case with Britten, Acting Head of Information there. He'd given me an oblique glance and advised,

> It's important to realise that we are not in the business of guilt and innocence, which would be nice in moral black-and-white terms... we're in the business of the safety of convictions.

I found this strange to say the least but we went on to clarify what was meant by a miscarriage of justice. 'A miscarriage surely means a failure on the part of the judiciary to reach the desired end result of "justice",' I insisted. I was seated opposite Britten who sat behind a desk in a huge room full of empty offices. I wondered where on earth all the staff were considering there should have been over ninety of them.

'Agreed, but the definition is still very large. A conviction can be quashed for instance on procedural grounds but the convict may still be guilty. It may be quashed because of the way the case was handled.'

Britten sipped a coffee, inviting me to admire the view of Birmingham from the twenty-first floor, where we were seated. I guessed him to be in his mid-forties, a quaint sort of man with a well-to-do expression of helpfulness, patience and blankness.

'Would you criticise the CA in cases where the CCRC do refer a case and it is still upheld?' I queried.

Although his background was in journalism he had been with the CCRC for over three years, ample time I figured to have some kind of working knowledge of the organisation.

'We would be reluctant in any way to publicly criticise the CA in the sense that although obviously we have our independence, we have to have a close working relationship. I think the chairman, Sir Frederick Crawford, is quite happy with the proportion of cases that are quashed. Our terms of reference are that we have to be satisfied that there is, quote, "a real possibility" that the CA would find the conviction to be unsafe. If half of the cases we went through were referred, it would be pretty sort of frightening and would mean the system must be deeply flawed.'

And racist, I thought to myself, as I continued: 'But I'm thinking of cases like Eddie Guilfoyle, Samar and Jawad, and Susie May too. A number of people feel as if the statutory framework, the Appeal Act, should be changed, so that where "a real possibility" exists that justice may have miscarried, reflects whether a case is referred or not. Rather than a real possibility that a CA would not uphold the conviction, because the CA seems to have a history of failure, in that they will already have rejected the case previously.'

Britten paused. 'I think I'd have to take the commission's collective view on this, rather than my own personal opinion. My own view is that there should certainly be more flexibility.'

'Then there are those many cases that get rejected such as Satpal Ram. Are you familiar with his case?'

Britten replied, 'Yes. I mean, on a personal note, I looked at the Ram case, and reading it I thought this guy definitely got a wrong deal. I think it took a great deal of "should we, shouldn't we?" going round the office. You know I even took a group of people from the commission to watch that theatre production about him? *Banged Up*, it was called. My view is that in different circumstances he may have got off with self-defence. But we did a very exhaustive examination and there was no way the CA would have quashed the conviction. Which does seem strange, you know.'

I stared back at him. 'It's not that strange; I guess it's simply the state of justice today.' I decided to change tack. 'Do you have much contact with Frederick Crawford?'

Britten smiled. 'Yes, I sit outside his office, which is why we're having this meeting down here. He's very suspicious of the media. He'll have retired by the time your book comes out. He doesn't like journalists at all – they're next to child molesters – I don't know up or down on the scale. It makes my job difficult sometimes.'

I hid my surprise at his choice of words, feeling dumbstruck. Was I being paranoid or had I just been tagged a child-molesting journalist? At least I now knew where all the staff must be. 'Do you wish you could be more open at times?' I grinned, suddenly feeling like an intruder and finding it hard to treat the whole interview seriously. I wondered how far I would get running up the stairs to Crawford's office before security got to haul me out.

'It's the whole ethos; we have difficulties because we operate under the Criminal Appeal Act, so we're only able to communicate the reason for referring, or not referring a case, to the applicant or their legal representative. If I were to tell you the reason, I would be committing a criminal offence. So it does make it difficult.'

I changed tack again. 'You're not a freemason are you?'

Britten smiled ruefully again. 'No.'

'What do you think about Frederick Crawford being a freemason? Does it have any tangible effect on the commission's relationship with any of the judges or perhaps cause a conflict of interest sometimes in the decision-making process?'

Britten looked as if I'd sworn unexpectedly at him and immediately asked me to turn my Dictaphone off. I complied but it did not stop him from suddenly peering round the office, wondering out loud if it could be bugged. Perhaps he was humouring me but I believe he looked ever so slightly nervous. I did not press him to answer the question.

I liked Britten and all in all had gleaned greater insight into the workings of the organisation. He agreed with me that a gulf existed that could be applied across the whole of the judiciary. It consisted of a total lack of consideration in the process of who got to dish out justice and how much of it. We agreed that change would indeed happen and that the setting up of the CCRC had been a good thing. But as far as I was concerned (and Britten certainly seemed to share some of my concerns), the CCRC, like the judiciary, still failed to deliver any semblance of redress for the majority of people who insisted they had been wrongfully convicted.

Satpal was out of prison, but on licence as a murderer. He had lost the best years of his youth and literally had no idea of where or how he was supposed to fit back in to life on the outside. It was a problem that the state deemed his and his alone. He had no identity other than as a murderer out on licence, no income, and family with which he was far from familiar. His mum had passed away during the time he had been held in prison after being recommended for release. It is fair to say that he had nothing, bar a community of people willing to help him adjust. But beyond friendship, none of us really knew how to provide the care that someone like Satpal now needed. He didn't trust anyone in authority and when encouraged to meet with a counsellor, he'd refused, desperately insisting that his friends help him adjust. The best nights' sleep he got were when he'd reached physical and mental exhaustion and could no longer stand up or speak, and even then he'd still try and sleep with one eye open if he could, as he insisted he'd learnt to do in prison. He ate erratically, often going whole days with no food, which did nothing to help him build up his health again.

Satpal tried holding a job down for a couple of weeks, painting and decorating for a friend of his, but he'd return to the house in the afternoon almost hysterical, obsessively clock-watching as evening approached and beside himself with anxiety. It was hard to understand but in many ways it was like trying to look out for someone who needed to relearn childhood skills. Much had changed in the sixteen years he'd been away. It was strange to switch from campaigning in order to have Satpal released, to working overtime in an attempt to keep him in one piece once he had been released. There was always the fact that if Satpal was attacked again and defended himself, or if he became involved in any kind of minor altercation during which the police were called, he would be faced with an automatic recall to prison. In this sense he was far from free and this only added to his frustrations of having to adapt to life on the outside without justice. I believe Satpal lost the will and the strength to fight on for justice once he was released. Unlike Robert Brown, who won his appeal, Satpal had been reluctantly released by a system that refused to acknowledge that his was a case of self-defence.

Mark Barnsley

The 8 June 1994 heralded the start of my nightmare. I was thirty-three years old, and my wife had recently given birth to our third daughter, Daisy. My career as a writer was beginning to do really well and I was going to be taking my family to the Lake District on holiday. I remember feeling happy and secure; my life was right on track with regard to my family, my friends and my writing.

On this particular day, I'd spent the morning writing. I was a respected outdoor journalist, having written for various national newspapers and magazines, including the *Guardian*, and was under contract to write two books in the Questa Publications 'Walking with Children' series. I was also a member of the Outdoor Writers' Guild, and Equipment Editor of *Climber*, Britain's oldest and most prestigious outdoor publication. Prior to writing, I have been a youth worker, wine lecturer, English (TEFL) teacher and an International Red Cross worker.

My partner, Sam, went out for a while on the day of 8 June. Before leaving, she suggested that I invite a close friend of ours, Jane Leathborough, to visit the newest addition to the family. It was a warm, sunny day in Sheffield and we both agreed it would be a good idea if I went out for a walk with the baby and maybe stopped somewhere for a drink with Jane.

The three of us went into The Pomona pub that day at about 2.30 p.m. I'd gone inside the premises to purchase two pints of beer, while Jane settled in the beer garden with the baby. A number of students, about fifteen in total, were also in the pub. Having just finished college exams, they had gone there with the specific intention of getting as drunk as they could, something they all succeeded in doing. Their behaviour was aggressive and to add to this they had been smoking cannabis. After kicking a fruit machine, causing the alarm to activate, the students left the bar area and went to sit in the beer garden nearby Jane.

While waiting for me to bring over their drinks, Jane was verbally abused, taunted and insulted by a number of the students. One of the girls said to her, 'Look at you, you sad cow.' Shocked, Jane went up to the students to complain about their behaviour but she received no apology. She sat back down. I wasn't present during this entire incident.

I walked into the beer garden shortly after and Jane told me what had happened. Wishing to avoid any trouble, we both dismissed the incident and decided to leave shortly afterwards. To leave the beer garden we had no option but to walk past the tables where the students were sat. We were both subjected to a torrent of verbal abuse, including comments like, 'You can fuck off, you wanker.'

At this point I too attempted to speak to the students about their behaviour. At no time did I raise my voice to them; I spoke in even, ordered tones, trying to explain that we were just ordinary people like them trying to have a quiet drink, and that there was no need to abuse us. I thought I'd get an embarrassed apology but the students responded by hurling more abuse at me, and I began to fear for my daughter's safety. I was told to 'piss off', 'fuck myself', and one female got up to insult me further, pushing me in the chest. Another student smirked and said, 'I'd like to fuck your baby.'

I started walking away in appalled disgust but I was again pushed in the chest; another student grabbed me by the arm joined by at least three more students.

I was deeply aware at this point that I might be attacked and I began to struggle to get away. The male I later learnt was called Sheperd started punching me repeatedly and other students joined in. I was hit over the head with a glass, which cut my head open as I was knocked forward, though I managed to stay on my feet. Dizzy and shocked, I had to bear the brunt of further punches and kicks from the students, now grouped around me.

Trying to protect my head from the blows and still bent forward, I saw an open knife drop from one of the students and slide across the floor under one of the benches. Horrified, I stared at the knife as hands started to reach for it. In genuine fear for my life I believed that once my attackers gained repossession of the knife, they would not hesitate to kill me with it.

My view of the knife became obscured by one of the students stooping in front of me who was able to pick it up. I reacted by grappling to try and gain possession of it and at this point my finger was cut, likely due to grabbing the blade, even though someone else held it. I was able to gain possession of the knife and tried to warn off my attackers, crying out, 'Get back, leave me alone.' A middle-aged woman, who at the time I presumed to be the landlady of the pub, came out and also shouted at the students to leave me alone. As I'd turned to face her, the angry mob jumped me again, striking me in the face and subjecting me to a further onslaught of punches, kicks and verbal abuse.

I turned away from the woman who'd called out, to run down the small ramp into the car park. The students continued to group around and attack me as I tried to get away.

Jane witnessed the violence continue unabated and later described what was happening. 'Maybe eight people came running out from where the tables were, down the ramp. They were trying to grab hold of him, hitting and shouting at him. He kept trying to run away. I was transfixed with shock and remember him stumbling against a car. As he was against it he was being punched and kicked. He was taking a really serious beating.'

Francis Holsman, an engineer at the scene, had stated that I had blood all over my face and on the back of my head. Another witness, ambulance-driver Victor Bruchlowskyj, stated, 'I saw a bunch of males and females who appeared to be fighting. I saw several of them attacking one man who fell to the floor.'

All this time I tried to make my way across the car park to escape the students but I was continually surrounded, punched and kicked. I still had the knife in my hand but at no time did I deliberately try to injure my attackers with it. Bleeding profusely and in extreme pain and distress I eventually reached the road. Still being beaten, I ran about twenty-five yards down Ecclesall Road, when student Simpson outran me and turned to stand in front of me. I was punched full in the face.

Julie Quigley, a credit controller who witnessed the attack, stated, 'I saw a man being chased by three other lads. The youth in the white T-shirt (Simpson) managed to grab hold of the front man (Mark) and he started hitting him.'

Sheperd then caught up too and jumped on me, knocking me

to the ground. I still had the knife in my hand and was pinned to the ground on my knees, with my face close to the ground and my arms stretched out in front of me. Sheperd had his arm around my throat. I repeatedly told the students to let me go and one of them (a girl called Duncan) also demanded that they release me.

Eventually Sheperd said that he would let me go if I agreed to let go of the knife and go home. Of course I readily agreed and Sheperd made me repeat it. I slowly loosened my hold on the knife and he began to get up off me, being pulled off me at the same time by Duncan, who was still shouting at him to let me go.

I left the knife on the ground and managed to get up. Jane was horrified by my appearance and described me as, '…a mess, a really funny colour, green and white. There was a lot of blood coming from his head, his face and hand. He was holding himself at an unnatural angle. He had like a hole in his head. He couldn't open his mouth as it was swollen.'

When I was finally able to stagger away I was dizzy with shock. I did not have any further contact with any of the students. At around 3.30 p.m., several police patrols arrived at the Pomona pub and found five of the students, each claiming to have been injured. Shortly afterwards, I was the only person to be arrested by South Yorkshire Police. They charged me with five counts of 'wounding with intent to cause grievous bodily harm, contrary to Section 18 of the Offences Against the Person Act'. The headlines of the local newspaper, *The Star*, the following morning read: 'Five stabbed for poking fun at girlfriend. Knifeman slashes students at pub.'

After being remanded in custody for over a year, I went to court. My trial lasted nearly three weeks. I was acquitted of three of the five offences with which I had been charged, but was convicted on two counts. I was also convicted of three lesser alternative offences (unlawful wounding), for which I was never charged. After waiting a further five and a half months, I was sentenced to twelve years concurrent on the Section 18 convictions, and five years concurrent for each of the lesser offences.

The prosecution case against me was unbelievable. It was said that the group of students were quietly enjoying a drink to celebrate the end of their exams and that I'd suddenly attacked them, despite having no history of aggressive behaviour, and having never met any of the students before. Prosecuting counsel claimed that I'd deliberately stabbed five of the students, none of whom were drunk, because I took offence to a remark made in my absence, by one of the group who was not injured at all. The remark was allegedly about the sunglasses being worn by Jane Leathborough.

According to the prosecution I am a monster who went berserk over some trifling remark and savagely attacked a group of harmless young people with a knife, in the most vicious and cold-blooded way. That is contrary to *all* the evidence. If I was that sort of maniac, is it likely that I'd have waited to the age of thirty-three before launching such an attack, while sober, in broad daylight and with my baby daughter?

That the prosecution was able to bring any convictions at all in this case is telling. The defence case is supported by every single independent prosecution witness and there were at least *sixty* witnesses to the incident, none of whom claimed to have seen me produce, threaten or stab anyone with a knife. Most witnesses saw me being beaten savagely and trying to escape a large number of attackers.

After I was arrested, I underwent a medical examination and was seen by a Dr Pyrgos. In the report he'd stated, 'In my opinion

Mr Barnsley sustained injuries to his head, nose, left eyebrow, chest, right hand, right knee and other parts of his body, during the episode of 8 June 1994. Examination of the right hand revealed a scar about three centimetres long... The injury to the right hand consisted of a laceration on the index finger... The scar appears due to a wound caused by a cut with a sharp instrument. X-rays of the nasal bones revealed slight deviation of the bones to the right... He probably sustained a fracture of the nasal bones. The description of the pain in the chest is consistent with either severe bruising or fractures of one or more ribs.'

In addition to this report, a dentist, Paul Wright, examined me and made the following statement. 'On 8 June 1994 Mr Barnsley was punched and kicked to the face and body. Together with other injuries one of the patient's front teeth (UR1) was knocked palatally and the restoration in the tooth, a crown, was loosened. The crown fell out approximately two weeks later. Several weeks later a fragment of the root became exposed through the gum. On examination I found fracture to right central incisor (UR1). Pain and swelling of the gum around this. The injuries sustained to UR1 are consistent with trauma caused by a blow to the face... This tooth is not restorable. To dislodge the crown and fracture the root would take considerable force... The injury is consistent with Mr Barnsley's explanation... Quite considerable force would have been required to fracture the crown... A punch, or an elbow, or a kick.'

Quotations taken from the prosecution witnesses themselves demonstrate clearly how I had no case to answer yet this did not stop the prosecution from acting out the motions of court action.

I was sober when I was attacked whereas the students were

drunk and some of them had also taken drugs. Student complainant Sheperd stated in evidence, 'I had three pints of Younger's No 3 bitter inside the pub and two brandies and lemonade, and a pint of No 3 and another brandy outside.' Another student complainant stated in evidence, 'I had around six pints of Younger's No 3 bitter to drink.' Student complainant Thomas admitted to drinking 'around six pints of lager'.

Four of the students committed perjury in court by denying that they had used cannabis. Dr A. R. W. Forrest, a medical practitioner and chemist, provided an analysis of the complainants' blood on 21 June 1995, after receiving serum samples from the Forensic Science Service. He stated, 'A screening test for the presence of cannabinoids yielded a positive result.' He went on to explain that 'Cannabinoids are compounds found in the human body after the use of cannabis-containing products. The results would be consistent with them having used cannabis sometime before the alleged assault... The possibility that they were under the influence of cannabis at the time of the alleged assault cannot be excluded...'

Dr Forrest, added, 'The minimum amount of cannabis to register a positive reading is one or two joints. All the figures are very generous to the students.'

Judge Baker remarked, 'The students have lied about their use of cannabis. No matter how you caution the jury it would still affect their opinion of the students' credibility.' However, rather than take action, instead he withheld Dr Forrest's findings from the jury, ruling the students' use of cannabis and the fact that they had lied in court, inadmissible as evidence.

I was the first person to be injured with a weapon and received by far the most serious injuries. Doctor M. D. B. Clarke (a consultant forensic physician) made a report of the injuries sustained by the students and in it stated that only 'slight to moderate force would have been required'. This report was not submitted to the court.

My injuries were supplied in the form of a notebook to the court as Exhibit 73. 'Wound on top of head. Deep cut above left eye. Cut to throat below left ear. Bruising to top of head. Large lump behind left ear. Nose may be broken. Bruise on left cheek. Bruise on chin. Bruising to neck and throat causing difficulty speaking. Bruising to arms, chest and stomach. Swollen mouth. Heavy bruising to right rib cage (may be cracked) causing coughing and breathing difficulty (one rib cracked or broken [added after visiting hospital]). Internal damage to right knee. Cuts and bruising to both knees. Bruising to legs. Deep cut to right index finger. Cuts to hands, fingers, and right wrist. Damage to teeth.'

Sheperd admitted to chasing after me and stated in evidence, 'I have no idea why I chased him, whether from frustration or for a laugh. I just went after him. I jumped on his back in the car park.' Other students were involved in the attack and left the Pomona pub before the police arrived. Despite numerous applications by my defence, the police insist that they are unable to locate them. Two of these untraceable students were on the same university course as some of the complainants.

CHARACTER REFERENCES

I have known Mark Barnsley for well over ten years and have been acquainted with him for longer. In this time I have found him to be of good character and temperament. I know Mark best as a lover of the outdoors, as a companion climber and fell walker, and someone with a great respect for the natural environment. I have always thought of him as a true Yorkshireman, being forthright yet friendly, honest, and with high expectations of his friends. He does not bear fools lightly but always respects the rights of others and remains courteous where others might lose their tempers. In this respect I am incredulous of the case being brought against Mark as I know him to be a cool and sober person, not prone to rash acts and holding nothing but contempt for the perpetrators of violence.

Dr D. McClean, Senior Lecturer in Palynology

I am a solicitor with the Supreme Court... I have known Mark for ten years... I cannot believe there to be any sound basis upon which to regard Mark as a danger to the public. Mark has always struck me as an honest, cheerful, intelligent, and straightforward person.

Mr R. Parry, Solicitor

He is intelligent, outgoing, well mannered and considerate. He is every inch the dedicated father, being selfless in the provision of an emotionally secure and socially stimulating environment for his children. In all the time (over twelve years) I have known Mark he has always demonstrated an admirable adult magnanimity and support towards his partner. Mark has that endearing mixture of sagacity, humility, and restfulness of the soul found in lovers of the outdoors. Mark has volunteered help to me in my former profession as a sports development worker. He exhibited the kindness, humour and patience needed to work successfully, whatever the demands of the client group. To conclude, Mark has my unreserved commendation regarding his good character as a friend; associate; employee; father; partner; writer; jazz buff and wit. His continued incarceration is a tragedy not only for himself, but for his friends, and most importantly his grieving partner and daughters.

Mr J. Lamb, Physiotherapist

I have known Mark for over twelve years, meeting him through a colleague at university. We have had a consistent friendship and have spent many enjoyable times together, especially since we both had families. We both enjoy walking in the Peak District and have often taken our families out for the day together. I have always found Mark to be a sociable and well-balanced person, who would always go out of his way to help me if I so needed. I have never seen him become violent or aggressive and he has always displayed a mild temperament. He is a good and patient father to his children, who he loves dearly.

Ms L. Heffer, Student Nurse

Mark Barnsley presented as a pleasant, intelligent, co-operative and articulate young man. He seems to have always enjoyed a very stable, mature, responsible and pleasant personality. In my opinion Mark Barnsley does not suffer from any form of mental illness. He has shown no evidence of disorder of personality of any type or degree. On the contrary, he has been described in quite positive terms as a man of principles and honour, being honest, responsible, reliable, with an even temper and respect for others.

Dr A. H. Solomon, psychiatric report

The police and prosecution service were able to secure convictions only because they suppressed, withheld and planted evidence. The jury did not receive the full facts of the case, and the court process was thus abused. The judge was extremely biased, willing to suborn perjury. Law lecturer Gus MacDonald, who analysed the summing up of the case, has said,

There is no way that the Judge offered an impartial and fair summing up of the situation. It is not acceptable, should not be acceptable, for a judge to swing the whole story, to re-tell the whole story in such a way that the jury is put on the spot thinking: 'That's a judge – he's an expert – he must know what he's talking about. If I can't make up my own mind I'll follow the hints he's given me. This guy must be really dangerous, he must be locked up, these students have a great future ahead of them.' The judge's summing up is a totally biased report. It's like an echo of the prosecution case, there's very little attempt to balance what the defence has to say.

APRIL 2002, HMP WHITEMOOR

Under British law a twelve-year prison sentence is made up as follows, for non-lifers: after six years, i.e. halfway through, the prisoner is eligible for release on parole. If parole is not granted, or as in my case not applied for (how can I be paroled for something I didn't do?), the prisoner will be automatically released after eight years. Until the early 1990s that was it, the prisoner's sentence was officially over. But now, after release, a prisoner is 'on licence' and during that period can be returned to prison at any time. For the next three years there is an 'at risk' period.

Despite my experiences of the British injustice system, I had always thought that I would be freed from prison through the Appeal Court, not simply thrown out on the streets after eight years, with my wrongful conviction still intact. For me it is a terrible thing, one I haven't even been able to bear thinking about.

Having rejected the parole procedure on principle, I thoroughly resent the idea of being released on licence. The conditions can be extremely draconian and such licences can be used as a means of targeting people for further fit-ups. They can be hauled back into prison at any time.

I won't be signing the licence so I don't know for certain what will happen when the time for my release comes. But I expect, if I am released, all my actions and movements will be closely monitored, scrutinised and controlled. I will still be a prisoner, albeit one with a longer chain. The uncertainty is extremely stressful not just for me but my family too. This summer I am due to be released from a maximum-security prison, where I currently spend more time locked in my cell than when I was first imprisoned eight years ago. For me there have been no 'home leaves', days out or any form of 'preparation for release'. It seems as if the state has deliberately attempted to inflict the maximum psychological and physical damage on me.

So am I looking forward to getting out? Of course I don't want to live in these dreadful conditions forever and I always hope for the day this nightmare will finally end. But freedom (such as it is) without justice does not have a sweet taste. I haven't seen the stars for eight years. I've never had a view from my cell that wasn't just concrete and razor wire and the only time I've been out of my cell after midnight was during the 1997 Full Sutton prison riot. But I view the whole idea of 'getting out' with some trepidation. I'll leave here jobless, homeless and penniless, eight years older, and with my health damaged. My burning thirst for justice remains unquenched.

The only sense of triumph possible is that I've managed to survive so far without being killed or driven to insanity. Will I always remember the smells of prison? The stink of filthy toilets, sheets and clothes that reek of someone else's sweat, the stench of fresh faeces being smeared on a block-cell wall?

JANUARY 2003

It's now six months since the gates of Whitemoor Prison opened and spat me back out onto the streets again. In many ways these six months have not been easy. Having succeeded in making me homeless even prior to my release, the harassment I have received from the state has been relentless. After I eventually found somewhere to live in Sheffield, the police intervened to make me homeless. At one stage I was literally living out of a rucksack, with the constant threat of re-imprisonment hanging over my head. I was eventually forced to abandon my plans to live close to my children in South Yorkshire, and moved to Leeds. Even after I had again found somewhere to live, the Probation Service took nearly two months to approve the address. It was only recently that I spent my first night in over eight years in my own bed. My homelessness has meant that I have not been able to do any sort of work, on my case or otherwise. I have not had access to my legal papers or to my few possessions. I have not even been able to answer mail sent to me prior to my release, and of course it has been very stressful.

Inevitably, eight years in high-security prisons, two of which were spent in solitary, with beatings, bad food and brutalisation have caused me health problems, and I have not yet managed to regain the fitness I once took for granted. Most seriously a proration problem caused by eight years of walking on hard flat prison exercise yards recently caused my tibia to snap in two. This meant a week in hospital, an operation to insert a steel rod inside my shin, and it has left me on crutches and housebound. For an ex-prisoner it is a cruelly ironic situation. I am unable to decorate my new flat, unable to get to see my children much, and I still spend too much of my time alone and locked behind my door.

Of course, despite the state harassment and the ongoing effects of eight years' wrongful imprisonment I have still had some great times in the past six months. I have really enjoyed meeting some of the people who wrote to me and supported me while I was locked away, and many have become close personal friends. Countless times I have been unable to stop myself grinning like a Cheshire cat at the thought of how much better than prison even the most ordinary situations are, just to be close to friends, and not to have some turn-key telling me to get behind my door.

There is still no word from the Criminal Cases Review Commission, but what's happened to me cannot simply be swept under the carpet. I won't be the last person that gets fitted-up. When I can walk again, I hope to continue meeting as many people as possible in my fight for justice. I thank everyone whose acts of kindness and friendship have helped to make my post-prison life easier than it might have been. The struggle continues.

7

THE NATURE AND DETAIL OF OPPRESSION

I used to think that once the CA had overturned a wrongful conviction, life would begin to get better again for those prisoners who regained their freedom. If a prisoner got out on parole first then they could continue to fight their conviction from the outside, which is surely better than continuing to suffer alone on the inside. Regrettably however this is not the case, for the hell prisoners have been forced to live in for so long has become the norm. Life beyond the prison wall for some, especially those who are imprisoned at a very young age, has come to mean absolutely nothing in real terms. Independence has been lost. The scars of time spent in prison affects innocent victims and their families for the rest of their lives.

On 31 December 2001, Dr Adrian Grounds, prominent university lecturer and Honorary Consultant in Forensic Psychiatry, based at the Institute of Criminology, Cambridge, finished writing up his latest assessment of Paddy Hill. It detailed his current condition in relation to the impact of imprisonment, ten years since his release. Dr Grounds originally assessed Paddy in July 1993 and has a wealth of experience in evaluating other wrongfully imprisoned individuals:

Paddy Hill: History Since 1993

At the time of the interview, June 2001, Mr Hill had been living in a two-bedroom flat in North London, where he had been residing for the last nine years. He lived alone, and was receiving Income Support of £75 per week. He had debts totalling £20,000.

Paddy had met numerous other prisoners while incarcerated who were also innocent. He helped fight for their release, and took victims of miscarriages of justice into his home, when they'd been dumped outside the prison gates or court with nowhere to live. When Johnny Kamara had his conviction overturned in March 2000 by the CA, he'd been left alone with six clear plastic bags containing his belongings, a £46 discharge grant and a travel warrant that expired that evening. Having spent twenty years in prison, he was completely disorientated by life on the outside and had no support from any official agencies. It had been a case of spend the night on the street or move in with Paddy.

> Paddy spends the majority of his time visiting prisoners, and works with six others who are involved with the Miscarriages of Justice Organisation (MOJO), which he founded. He has his own car and said that driving alone is the only activity that gives him a sense of freedom

and solace. He frequently drives for hours at night. This is linked with his chronic inability to feel relaxed and settled.

Paddy reported that he had been in reasonably good physical health, apart from having long-term problems with blocked nasal passages following an injury in HMP Winson Green.

In his book, *Forever Lost Forever Gone,* Paddy describes how he came to receive such an injury. Pulling up to the reception block in a big van surrounded by prison officers and armed police, he and the other members of the Birmingham Six had been kicked out onto the floor. Paddy was grabbed by the arms and frog-marched into the prison reception area.

'Because I hadn't signed a statement they told the screws I should be given extra special treatment, and a cop gave me a sharp kick between the legs as an example. Then the screws, loads of them by now, just went completely crazy attacking us. I was punched and kicked across the room and ended up supporting myself against a small swing door that led into the bath area. It was made of wood and only about four feet high. Somebody grabbed me by the hair and smashed my face down on top of the door. My nose burst apart and the blood ran from it like a tap. There was blood everywhere, all over my shirt and soaking my chest and stomach. A screw told me to keep my head up because the blood was making a mess on the floor.'

Dr Grounds' report continues:

> Mr Hill had received outpatient psychiatric and psychological help from Dr Mackeith and Dr Gudjonsson at the Maudsley Hospital, London between 1992 and 1995. Since then he has not had regular psychiatric follow-up but he continues occasionally to telephone Dr Mackeith. Mr Hill's outpatient attendance was erratic and he was only seen on a few occasions, often with long intervals between. He therefore cannot be said to have had any sustained courses of treatment. When Mr Hill attended as an outpatient, Dr Mackeith and Dr Gudjonsson noted his very high levels of tension, anger and anxiety. He was prescribed antidepressant medication (Amitriptyline). He took this for about two months and then stopped because he did not like taking tablets.

> In the interview, Mr Hill reported chronic symptoms of tension, rage, anxiety, depressed mood and sleep impairment. At times he was very low in mood and tearful. He described difficulties in getting to sleep and a fitful sleeping pattern. Frequently he would wake up feeling very tense and angry. He experienced high levels of subjective tension that were relieved by taking cannabis. He said that without the drug he would be extremely tense and aggressive.

He continued to experience panic attacks characterised by feelings of subjective terror, sweating and hyperventilation. Seeing police officers precipitates the panic attacks, and he continues to be highly apprehensive and fearful that he might be stopped by police officers and taken into custody. Mr Hill described continuing problems of irritability, episodes of explosive anger and marked mistrust of others.

PSYCHIATRIC EXAMINATION

Mr Hill was co-operative, tense and talkative in interview. Despite a superficially sociable and engaging manner, he was low and despairing in mood. He reported significant depressive and anxiety symptoms. There was no evidence of any psychotic symptoms or cognitive impairment.

At the time of my assessment nine years ago, Mr Hill showed evidence of three psychiatric disorders. He had a persistent and disabling mood disorder characterised by tension, anxiety, anger, and depression. Secondly, he had post-traumatic stress disorder. Thirdly, the accounts of Mr Hill and his family indicated a significant and persistent change in his personality characterised by a marked estrangement from others (enduring personality change after catastrophic experience). There were substantial difficulties in his family relationships. I thought he was likely to need long-term outpatient psychiatric support and treatment, including courses of specific medication for depression, and psychological treatment for his tension and post-traumatic stress symptoms. There also appeared to be a need for family therapy to assist Mr Hill and his immediate family with the tasks of adjustment and gaining mutual understanding.

The most striking finding in the current assessment is that there has been no substantial improvement in Mr Hill's condition. He continues to suffer from a chronic mood disorder and post-traumatic stress disorder. The changes in his personality and his estrangement from others remain. He has not been able to sustain intimate and close relationships with others, and he remains disabled by chronic tension and anger. The substantial damage done to Mr Hill's capacity to experience and maintain intimate relationships with others leaves him isolated and this is likely to continue. In effect, he has lost his capacity to enjoy family life.

Overall, Mr Hill's psychiatric difficulties are of the same severity as when I saw him nine years ago and it is likely that he will remain permanently disabled by them.

Over the course of the last ten years, Dr Adrian Grounds had made psychiatric assessments of thirteen other men who have been wrongfully convicted and sent to prison. He remains appalled that, given his findings, to date there is still no organised system of professional help available for those released on appeal.

Dr Grounds' report concluded,

> A major aspect of Mr Hill's chronic anger and bitterness is the absence of any official apology for his wrongful imprisonment. In my experience, amongst those who have been wrongfully imprisoned, the need to have an apology, an official response of regret and acknowledgment that they were wronged, is of the greatest psychological importance. Commonly, these people feel this to be more important than money, and the absence of such responses maintains intense bitterness.

Out of all the victims of miscarriages of justice that Dr Grounds had evaluated, it became clear that among his clinical findings there was significant

> ...enduring personality change after catastrophic experience.

The key feature of the condition was observable as

> ...inflexible and maladaptive characteristics that impair interpersonal, social and occupational functioning.

Characteristics included

...a hostile or mistrustful attitude towards the
world, social withdrawal, feelings of emptiness
and hopelessness, a chronic feeling of threat, and
estrangement.

Other psychiatric disorders included anxiety attacks,
paranoia and depression.

In many of the cases Dr Grounds had studied, there
were reports of assaults and beatings, verbal threats,
deprivation of food and sleep and exhaustion. The terror
of being assaulted or killed added to the psychological
distress associated with living day to day with the
knowledge of being wrongfully convicted and
unsuccessfully trying to overturn the conviction. It was
not uncommon for cases to demonstrate intense, chronic
feelings of bitterness, and powerful, unresolved feelings
of loss. Victims of injustice described to Dr Grounds how
they had learnt to deal with the emotional pressures and
stresses of prison by suppressing painful feelings, avoiding
communication and isolating themselves. This kind of
coping strategy, perhaps useful in prison, continued after
release and was often inappropriate, making it almost
impossible to sustain new social relationships.

———————

Twelve years on since the release of the Birmingham Six,
I am chatting to Paddy in his office in Farringdon, watching
a huge parrot fly around the room. Paddy tears off a piece
of the sandwich he is eating and holds it out to the bird,
mumbling softly to it. It gingerly accepts, squawking delight
at the offering. Leroy walks over, laden with coffees. He'd
done time with both Paddy and Satpal and they've been

close friends ever since. It's been about two months since Satpal was released and I admit to them that he's been high as a kite and partying hard ever since.

'He might head exactly the way Gerry Conlon did,' Paddy remarks with a worried scowl, 'and he's not such a significant miscarriage of justice in the sense that he was at least present at the scene of the crime and had knowledge of it.'

For Paddy, coming out of prison had been just as traumatic as all the years he had endured in prison. Leroy looked up at him. 'The circumstances are different and unique in every miscarriage-of-justice case.'

I felt speechless as I tried hopelessly to imagine what was worse, sipping my coffee. Being plucked off the street, beaten nearly to death and having twenty-one life sentences wrapped round your neck? Or being stabbed during dinner, defending yourself thinking you might bleed to death at any minute, and having one life sentence wrapped round your neck? The judge had told Paddy and his co-defendants that they were never, ever to be released. The thought of being sent to prison either way made my blood run cold.

Paddy reached for his pipe. 'It's only about a year or so after you get out, if you have the guts and the intelligence to admit it to yourself, that you realise how fucked up and really alone you are. Many people turn straight to hard drugs and alcohol because they can't face up to being out of prison. They can't recognise the outside world. The babies they remember have all grown up and a whole generation of family life has come and gone forever.'

They tell me about Gerry Conlon of the Guildford Four. 'He had nowhere to go and there was no provision for him by the state. He came out with no money, no counselling, no references and no identity. Gareth Pierce gave him and Judith Ward accommodation at her place for six months. Like many of us Gerry turned to alcohol and drugs. There were lots of things that he couldn't get out of his mind, like seeing people in prison kill themselves and the beatings he endured. One day you realise that the drugs don't work and hopefully you stop taking them. He still has nightmares about being stripped, spat and urinated on.'

Leroy had accompanied me to Bolton to meet up with Paul Blackburn and I'll always be glad. I remember Paul trying to explain, with tears in his eyes, how the mental torture never stopped and how the resistance that he'd built up over the years in order to cope remained with him every single hour of every single day. While spending time with Rob Brown in Glasgow, it wasn't difficult to see how a quarter of a century of confinement had taken its toll – he would break into bouts of compulsive pacing. His behaviour wasn't unlike that of the caged tigers that are rescued by the Born Free Foundation and released into the wild to start new lives.

Rob had two perfectly decent bedrooms to sleep in but preferred to sleep on the floor of his living room. He'd insisted that he would be one of the few victims of injustice who would get on with his life though. Rob believed that innocent prisoners that had built up a lot of public support over the years had to be careful not to become delusional once they were released. Now that he was out of prison, he had people in the street greeting him all of the time, recognising his face in the newspapers and calling him a working-class hero. He didn't want to be raised onto any kind of platform, he just wanted to be himself, yet he also recognised the need to educate the public about the plight of innocent prisoners, from first-hand experience. Having watched other high-profile victims of injustice emerge from prison over the years, he'd concluded that many had had no idea of the effect that media (and subsequently public) interest would have on them. It was all too easy to get caught up in the public euphoria of release and harbour false notions of grandeur or fame. The higher the profile of the case, the more media attention the prisoner received upon release.

Most innocent people have no idea of how to attach value to money after being in prison for a long time. Interim compensation payments and emergency welfare funds (often raised by hardworking campaigners) have been burnt away on champagne, whiskey, cocaine and ecstasy. On one occasion when Rob visited Leicester Square in London, he stayed out from eleven p.m. to five a.m. giving money away to every homeless person he saw in the street. It meant nothing to him because money couldn't ever bring back twenty-five years of his life, or his mother's. But when he'd stood back to think about it, he realised that money would give him a better of quality of life – if he was in control.

———————

The Chief Inspector of Prisons Anne Owers has recently described a number of prisons in England and Wales as being totally unacceptable.[1] HMP Liverpool has been described as having cockroach infestations, broken windows, blocked drains and dirty toilet facilities. Inmates are allowed to shower and change their clothes just once a week. Many of the single cells house two prisoners who have to share an unscreened toilet. In 1999 Owers discovered that only eighteen per cent of prisoners had access to education though ninety-five per cent had basic literacy and numeracy difficulties. During her visit to the prison in 2003, she was dismayed to find that opportunities for education had declined even further.[2]

At HMP Wandsworth suicide attempts by inmates are becoming a frighteningly regular occurrence. In May 2003 during the heat-wave one prisoner wrapped himself up in his clothes and set himself on fire with a lighted match. By the time prison officers dragged him out he had been severely burnt. Despite temperatures in the high eighties, inmates were being locked up in their cells for the night by 3.30 p.m. with not even a drink of water to sustain them until the morning. Seventy-three per cent of prisoners on 'basic regime' were black, though forty-five per cent of the 800 inmates were black.

In the last five years there have been over 400 self-inflicted deaths in prisons in England and Wales. Although women make up only six per cent of the population, they account for eleven per cent of the suicides. Almost *all* women who have had to deal with being separated from their children have tried to harm themselves. They've used scouring pads and hairgrips to cut themselves – one young woman succeeded in choking to death by swallowing toilet tissue.

Two-thirds of all women in prison are now suffering from a mental disorder according to the Prison Reform Trust. In January 2003 at HMP Styal, where Sue Lucas-MacMillan exists, an eighteen-year-old, Sarah Campbell, killed herself by taking an overdose. She'd been at the prison for a day. In April a twenty-four-year-old, Jolene Willis, was found hanged in her cell. In June forty-one-year-old Hayley Williams was found hanged. Campaigners are calling for an independent enquiry into Styal Prison as the number of suicides has now risen to seven in the past ten months.

The definition of oppression is prolonged cruel treatment. We can choose to identify with it and learn to recognise it in its various shapes and forms if we want to. The world has never been so wide-open to us all as it is in 2004 and the ability we have to share experiences with others has never been greater. In fact sharing experiences is a must if we are ever truly to have a system capable of delivering justice as a principle objective. Doesn't any subject become personal if it concerns persons? We mustn't be put off by wigged arrogance. How much longer do we wish to live in a world where lying is to be considered an art form favoured by the state? For how much longer are British people prepared to be set up for judgement by arrogant liars?

The state today is made up of a number of individuals in dominant positions of power who ought to be challenged, considering the kind of pay-cheques they collect – and that includes MPs. Every time someone innocent of a crime is sentenced to prison, we learn how powerful those people are when it comes to being able to destroy. Judiciary or executive, it's all the same, just a seemingly impenetrable web of power. We are taught to fear and excuse the system, because the people in power are so good at disregarding and totally ignoring the human pain generated by their actions. It is the number-one hallmark of power. On a global level it works in exactly the same way. Iraq won't jump to the tune of the USA and Britain so her people are getting hurt. The message is, do what we say or we will lock you up, maim you and kill you. We saw how many bombs they dropped – but dead people are 'regrettable', that's all. A whole country in ruin is merely regrettable. Lying has become an art form and on that basis, the government can do what it likes because lying and democracy don't go hand in hand.

It's obvious, isn't it? We could never possibly build enough prisons, hire enough police officers, increase enough prison sentences or lock up enough people to prevent crime from happening. The current system actually generates crime by dehumanising people and acting as though it is acceptable behaviour. And we wonder why the youth of today is so disaffected. Personally, I'm surprised and very respectful of the fact that far more of our dear youngsters aren't gun-toting raving lunatics. We have government ministers proving to us all that crime really does pay – if you can afford it. Who could blame our easily influenced youth for gaining an unhealthy interest in bombs or bullets after the war with Iraq? They look to us for guidance and this is how we show them to behave when we don't get what we want.

Of course there are youths that are badly affected and seriously harmed by the environments in which they grow up – especially if one of their parents has been wrongfully convicted of a serious crime. The children of wrongfully convicted prisoners abruptly lose family stability and face huge disruption to their family unit. For those convicted prisoners who then mount a campaign to prove their innocence, a single parent on the outside and the children may have to bear the brunt of negative, extremely damaging publicity from the media. They may become ostracised and excluded from their communities.

While the remaining parent may sink into deep depression, children are inevitably left with even less family support at the very time that lifeline of support is critical. They may be excluded from school as they struggle to cope with bullies. With unsympathetic teachers they may develop behavioural problems. They are often left emotionally distraught and can be psychologically damaged for life. In the worst-case scenarios, where a family unit is forced to turn to state benefits following a wrongful conviction, the affected child becomes lost in a downward spiral into poverty, distress, mental illness, abuse and neglect. Some will turn to drugs to cope and then to drug-dealing or petty crime to pay for the 'escape'.

Rather than nurture a vision of law that rehabilitates the drug addict or which protects and supports the vulnerable single mother we are somehow expected to respect and appreciate Labour's latest get-tough-on-the-family tactics. If you can't pay the TV licence fee, you will be locked up for a futile spell. The government is not interested in matching the punishment to the crime by simply taking away the offending television – that would involve way too much brainpower and compassion. Similarly, when a vulnerable single parent can't force her troubled child to attend school she gets taken away and locked up too. Sensible and logical? Only in our wildest nightmares.

Not satisfied with convicting a proportion of British parents for non-serious crimes in order to give the family unit a good bashing, the age at which children can be remanded in custody for non-serious crimes has now been lowered to twelve. The United Nations Committee on the Rights of the Child cannot understand why the government would wish to incarcerate and incriminate hundreds more children in secure units. Pilot schemes have so far resulted in hundreds of older teenagers being moved into young-offender institutions while the oldest youth have been squashed into overfilled adult prisons.

According to Dr Michael Naughton, a researcher at the Department of Sociology at the University of Bristol, the miscarriage-of-justice problem has risen to an annual average of 3,750 known cases. In May 2003 proposed reforms of the Criminal Justice Bill were debated in the House of Commons but not one person offered proposals for reform through the eyes and experiences of Britain's miscarriages of justice. There was no mention of any of the issues surrounding wrongful conviction in the present system, or of reducing the numbers occurring. Instead the harm caused to victims of injustice is being swept under the carpet while government ministers attempt to make it even easier for the police and the prosecution to convict more people.

---

1 *The Independent*, 3 June 2003.
2 *BBC News Online*, 28 May 2003.

8

WHAT DOES THE FUTURE HOLD?

Members of Parliament, Ministers and Legislation

This haphazard journey around some of the various agencies and prisons of the criminal justice system has led me back to the House of Commons in 2003, to attend MOJO's second annual meeting. In two years I feel as though I've barely scraped the surface of the issues involved for victims of serious miscarriages of justice. I am heartened by the fact that some victims of miscarriages of justice, albeit a minority of them, walk back out into freedom via the Court of Appeal – for this proves to me that corrupt structures can be challenged successfully, against all odds. An exonerated prisoner in the form of Robert Brown has filled me with hope for a better future, odd as that may sound. When we consider that on one side you have the caged prisoner, and on the other you have the powerful might of the state, every successful appeal hints that corrupt structures are also vulnerable.

Having read the stories of the prisoners featured here, we realise that what has actually been told to us are two conflicting stories that challenge the status quo of legal thought. There are only two possible conclusions to these stories – either these people are liars, or those people responsible for the maintenance of criminal justice are deeply deluded.

My biggest realisation has been that much of the public know very little about the intricate workings of our criminal justice system, though most of us retain the strong belief that it doesn't function productively. We want to rebalance the justice system in favour of 'the victim' – those who are harmed by crime – yet to do it we are led to believe that it is necessary to take away the human rights of all defendants. There are recurring myths that never seem to be willingly dispelled, as when, for example, most people still believe that defendants must have done something wrong in order to end up in court, or in prison. We believe that all prisoners will try and say that they are innocent in order to get out of prison, and most of us will gladly advocate sending people to prison, though we've never stepped inside one before and have no idea what goes on inside them, or what they do to people.

In a speech to students last year, Metropolitan Police Commissioner Sir John Stevens accused the legal system of favouring the accused. He said there was a real danger of civil unrest unless the criminal justice system was radically overhauled to stop the guilty walking free. Yet, as a society we already jail more people in Britain than any of our counterparts in Western Europe. The prosecution achieves a conviction rate of over ninety-five per cent of defendants in our magistrates' courts, where over ninety-eight per cent of criminal trials are currently conducted. Over eighty-seven per cent of defendants in the Crown Court (where the remaining two per cent of cases are heard) are also found guilty. So once criminal suspects have been arrested or charged, the overwhelming majority of cases *do* result in conviction. While this does not rule out the possibility that many guilty offenders aren't brought to justice, it does lead me to question how fair the commissioner's comments are.

One of our deepest concerns should lie with the fact that the criminal justice system is ineffective when it comes to bringing corrupt police officers to justice, and is therefore inadequate in playing its part in maintaining a police force of integrity. As far as I can see, the only real danger of civil unrest occurs through a more pronounced distrust in the police forces as time goes by. There is no doubt that the criminal justice system fails whenever it acquits the guilty. But it fails every single one of us too whenever it convicts the innocent and the failure is greater because if we don't value our right to liberty then what point is there in placing value on anything?

I have tried to listen to as many people as possible, whose experiences of criminal justice have led them to voice their concerns. I subsequently learnt that wrongfully convicted people have been for the most part ignored in current debates about criminal justice. Victims of crime must include those who are wrongfully convicted if we are to talk about improving criminal justice. The reality is that miscarriages of justice are a prominent feature of today's system and thus any debate about reform that excludes this section of victims, is unjustifiable and without foundation. Restricting our right to trial by jury or allowing our fingerprints to be retained permanently on the national database or ending the 'double jeopardy' rule are all issues that have no bearing on protecting our freedoms and acquitting the innocent while convicting those guilty of crimes. The issues we need to debate include the ongoing dilemma over disclosure rules and the fact that forensic evidence may be seriously flawed. We desperately need to focus on getting innocent people out of prison and we also need to question why a greater proportion of corrupt police officers are not brought to justice. If a culprit cannot be found for a crime, is it right to put immense pressure on the police and label them as failures?

In the House of Commons I listened to John McDonnell talk about his experiences and how he came to be involved in the field of miscarriages of justice. Few MPs have proved as supportive, willing not only to listen but also to respond to people's concerns.

> Twenty years ago I was arrested in Parliament Square. I was the Chair of Finance of the GLC (Greater London Council) and walking to County Hall. A group of women who were part of the Greenham Common Peace Movement started singing in front of me and they all got arrested. Their legal adviser handed me their names on a list and asked me to get another lawyer for them. So the police arrested me. I got thrown into a van and taken up to Kennington Jail. In court three members of the police patrol group

gave different stories of the events that had happened. I was astounded to learn that I'd run along the road for about fifty yards, leapt over a fence, jumped onto an officer's back and punched a number of them! The police made serious allegations which carried a custodial sentence and which would have ruined my life had I been found guilty. Luckily, there was an American tourist who had an old-fashioned camera at the demonstration and who had managed to video the whole incident. We were all released but not one officer was brought to book for the perjury on that case.

Six months after his release he'd been approached by relatives of Paul Hill of the Guildford Four. McDonnell believes that the time has come to set up an all-party group on miscarriages of justice, in which MPs would be brought together to secure justice and redress for some of the thousands of individual cases clogging up the system. I wish him luck with the task of breathing life into those many MPs who usually pass the buck because their loyalties (and ultimately the mortgage) lie with party policy and promotion rather than their constituents. Hope is the thing that keeps most of us getting up in the morning though. Perhaps if we persist in the education of our MPs we really can influence party policy for the better. It is up to concerned members of the public to do so.

In the interests of justice it is vital that an *independent* investigation takes place to investigate allegations of police corruption. For those who have since had their convictions quashed at the CA it is just as vital. Once evidence of corruption comes to light, the criminal justice system should immediately arrange for the investigation of the police officers involved and issue an unreserved apology to the wrongfully convicted, with a public statement acknowledging the *innocence* of the appellant. It's time judges in Britain moved beyond addressing the technical 'safety' of a conviction and had the guts to apologise to its devastated victims of injustice. Until this happens, society is going to deteriorate further into a captive, police state.

If judges are shown to be overwhelmingly reluctant to use their powers via the appeals process in the face of blatant evidence, then what are we meant to do with them? How do we respect them? What use do they serve? They become part of the process that actually generates crime by keeping innocent people in jail and real-life killers at large. Judges have names and addresses, do we not have the right to question their decisions and judge them accordingly? An independent body ought to be able to monitor the performance of each individual judge and sack him or her for incompetence just as occurs in virtually every other profession.

Nick Taylor and Michael Mansfield are of the opinion that if the CCRC reasonably believes that a miscarriage of justice has occurred then it should recommend a re-trial. If the court of appeal refuses then the commission should have the ability to recommend that a conviction be quashed (unless the judges could provide a reasonable case otherwise) – the onus would then be weighted in favour of acquittal.

With the CCRC presently referring just 3.6 per cent of its caseload it is clear that its commissioners are still not getting to the crux of the matter in most instances though. Part of the reason is that the commission still depends on the police to carry out re-investigations of its cases. As such, I am left wondering how many years it will take for people like Sue Lucas-MacMillan and Keith Li to be reunited with their children, if at all. How much longer will it take Paul Blackburn, Mark Barnsley and Satpal Ram to get acquitted, if at all? Will Stephen Hector ever get the paperwork he needs to find out how he came to be convicted? I wonder if Annie Walsh and her family will ever get justice and if Annie Walsh rests in peace with at least the knowledge that an innocent man has been acquitted of her murder a quarter of a century later.

Who among us is willing to provide support for Sue Lucas-MacMillan, Keith Li and Paul Blackburn, who for years have been saying 'I am innocent and I need someone to help me prove it.'? There are thousands of others like them. I am not saying that everyone is to be believed and released – only that everyone deserves a chance to be listened to. Every case deserves a detailed, rigorous evaluation, given the significant risks of convicting innocent people.

There is no doubt that government initiatives can have an impact upon crime levels, but not if the agenda of the day involves making war with other nations, without evidence of justification. Violence will breed violence and if our jails are anything to go by, the larger we permit our prison population to grow, the more fragmented, angry and anti-social our society as a whole will become. Between 1992 and 2002, the number of women prisoners rose from about 1,300 to well over 4,000, and an estimated 8,000 children are now affected each year as a result of their mothers' imprisonment. An unstable family upbringing and economic deprivation are factors that contribute to the causes of crime and so the government responds by obsessing over racist border controls to create an even larger section of society that is deprived of benefits and the right to work. In an attempt to cope with the government's criminalisation of people, the police regularly use harsher measures against the black community and courts hand down tougher sentences to black people.

Britain's obsession with sending people to jail has sadly meant that the idea of a fair trial no longer exists. Lord Chancellor Irvine, head of the judiciary, should have been someone who defended notions of due process and fair trial, but according to Jane Hickman, although he was the person responsible for funding Legal Aid, he said nothing on the subject for over five years. Lord Irvine's idea of a noble cause worth defending involved spending £650,000 of public money decorating his flat at the House of Lords, while sending people to jail gradually took priority over the protection of the public and the integrity of the system. He was also the person responsible for appointing our old, white, male, clone-like Oxbridge judges to reside over our diverse and multi-cultural population.

But wait. Just as I feel ready to consider opting out of life anywhere near the vicinity of governments and the criminal justice system, I feel change in the air. Tony Blair recently announced the abolition of 1,400 years of tradition; the role of the Lord Chancellor has been declared defunct (not before time), and Blair now feels like setting up a new American-like supreme court in place of the law lords as well as an independent judicial appointments commission. Lord Irvine has just resigned to make way for Lord Falconer in a new role as Minister of State for Criminal Justice. The battle to educate Lord Falconer about the issues of miscarriages of justice is declared open.

As if Home Secretary Blunkett's confused ramblings over criminal justice reforms were not enough to give us the heebie-jeebies, let's not forget that Falconer was the minister for that spectacularly expensive financial flop, the Millennium Dome. Why oh why did they have to pick the old Cambridge boy most closely associated with doggedly throwing bank vaults of our cash at that monstrosity, to pick up the dangling reins of something as monstrous as our system of justice? Between the two of them I have no doubt the initials HMP before Dome would be considered an attractive two-for-one package-solution in the scheme of things.

Protest Letters and Supporting Campaigns and Prisoners

I feel we have never before so badly needed to bring about a collective, inclusive, organised movement to bring about the right kind of change to the criminal justice system and the social order on a wider scale. Wise to the injustices and suffering experienced by serious miscarriages of justice, urgent support is needed for those families caught in the ever-widening ripple effect. The good news is that there is plenty we can be doing to help.

A brief trip back in history and there are suddenly millions of us marching against the war in Iraq because ultimately we perceive a threat to our quality of life. Okay, so it wasn't enough to restore any semblance of democracy or sanity to this run-away, profit-driven government of ours, but the debate about the war still goes on today and the issues are far from closed. As long as innocent blood is shed, people always find a way to rise up and stand beside each other, facing the threat, or the 'enemy'. That so many people could feel so strongly about a war in Iraq tells me that we are not the desensitised, unshockable population that we sometimes perceive ourselves to be. Apathy and silence, every dictator's good friend and the means by which routine conformity is bred into our lives, has temporarily fled from Britain. I give thanks for the internet, which I believe to be partly responsible for chasing them away.

People are not without a voice in this country, thanks to the ever-growing consolidation of previous protest movements, and too many people now require the government to be willing to listen to factual concerns, learn from them and be committed to respond accordingly. Our changing expectations are such that a lack of transparency in any system these days is a cause for protest and great concern. So we should feel free to insist on justice for all. Justice for the prisoners represented in this book is justice for each and every one of us. It definitely helps to write to your MP, care of the House of Commons, London, SW1A 0AA. Thanks to John McDonnell they can now join an all-parliamentary group of MPs on miscarriages of justice.

Then there's the Director of Public Prosecutions who ought to be encouraged to take responsibility for prosecuting corrupt police officers and permitting the equal disclosure of evidence on both sides of a case. Words, cheap and easy as they are and neatly wrapped up as promises, have come to mean absolutely nothing. In fact the Police Complaints Authority is finally in the process of being disbanded due to its lack of transparency. Pressure groups like Liberty, Justice, Legal Action Group, Miscarriages of Justice UK, the Lawrence Inquiry, Charter 88, the Institute of Race Relations, United Friends and Family and a host of other organisations with moral integrity, have the trust of local communities and the legitimacy to represent people's interests on their side. It's amazing what people can achieve when the circumstances warrant it.

From 31 March 2004 the Police Complaints Authority ceased to exist and was replaced by the Independent Police Complaints Commission (IPCC). Nick Hardwick is the chair and has stated that the IPCC will have the powers and resources to investigate complaints separately from the police service. Its eighteen commissioners, which, by law, must not have worked for police forces previously will be able to investigate incidents of alleged police misconduct separately from the direction and control of police forces. At the moment Hardwick spends his time listening and learning from the various bodies and organisations that have an interest in the commission. It's an ideal time to approach him, attend public meetings on miscarriages of justice and strengthen campaigns by taking the time to join them. Every single person helps, especially in cyberspace, and the internet has become the ideal tool for campaigning and mobilising support.

Home Secretary David Blunkett can be reached at the Home Office, 50 Queen Anne's Gate, London SW1 9AT. While I do not believe he is capable of responding to public needs, he shouldn't be left out of the action. Alternatively write to the British Ambassador if you live abroad and you can also write to the newspapers. The newly inaugurated National Miscarriage of Justice Day took place on 12 October 2003, almost a year since Robert Brown stepped out into freedom with over a hundred people marking the event in Liverpool. Similar events took place up and down the country.

Is there a limit to what people on the outside of the criminal justice system can do, once concerned citizens have aired their views? At some point perhaps there will come a time when a minority of people within the system itself will be willing to sit down with the Law Society and the Bar Council to discuss the notion of refusing to uphold the system any longer unless the issues of miscarriages-of-justice cases are redressed and individual case histories scrutinised from start to finish? Surely it only needs the will of a few more people to demonstrate what really matters to us in Britain – if the war in Iraq is anything to go by. If it's going to take an experienced lawyer sixteen years to get a wrongful conviction overturned, in the face of overwhelming evidence, what difference does it make to drop a case temporarily for a week or two in favour of collective negotiations with those responsible for running such a system? There are hundreds of cases that could be cited to the press. As far as I am aware, in the history of the legal profession there hasn't been much in the way of industrial action – but the increasing loss of human dignity, the erosion of fair working conditions and the disintegration of social stability have a habit of leading to volatile political circumstances.

If all the convicted people represented in this book are living within the truth, then they have all paid a savage penalty for speaking their minds. The very nature of their words challenges the power of the state and the judiciary and invites trouble. All the people who collaborate to place or keep innocent people behind bars, I believe do so for nothing more than careerism: power and personal gain. Contact with the criminal justice system may start with the police, but it certainly doesn't end there. In view of this it isn't shocking to find that notorious careerists and opportunists currently occupy so many political and influential job positions. Has Lord Falconer, by accepting the post of Criminal Justice Minister, now persuaded himself that his work ahead will actually rescue anybody from the wrongful clutches of the criminal justice system? I think not.

So where does that leave people like me, forced to be a hypocrite by paying my taxes? By putting together this book will I be an object of ridicule, to be played down or ignored altogether alongside these prisoners? Such pessimistic behaviour becomes normal when we conform. And believe me, I do understand it because funnily enough I'd rather be gardening in my back yard and happily paying my taxes than visiting people in maximum-security hell-holes and thinking of myself as any kind of hypocrite.

But if people in prison are innocent and there is almost no one in the criminal justice system willing to help them, doesn't that mean that our society is somehow upside down and inside out? That the real mission of law and order today can't possibly be to protect the free development of mankind from criminal activity, but that it really exists to protect criminal activity from the hazard that the free development of mankind poses? Why else would the cruel and unnecessary banishment of so many lives into Britain's prisons be taking place? We all have to pay for it in the form of a slow yet steady decline in the spiritual and moral integrity of society as a whole. And if we decide that miscarriages of justice are a sad but necessary occurrence in society because law and order (if only superficial) must be maintained, regardless of how it is acquired, then what does that say about us? As long as we are prepared to ignore people in prison who insist that they are innocent, we have to ask ourselves: what profound and moral impotence will Britain be suffering from tomorrow?

One thing I know to be true is that history has a habit of demanding to be heard. We can put human beings through a very precise and exhaustive process of violation, paralysis and the denial of social time. But one day the truth comes back to haunt us. It may take ages, but eventually it happens; the walls start to crack and the locks are no longer strong enough. Those prisoners who dare to cry out words of truth and stand behind them with every inch of their souls cannot be denied forever. Suddenly the dead-weight of oppression crumbles and history appears once again to take its place. The masks worn by those in authority are suddenly dropped and the colossal system of collective power breaks down into individual people. We wake up one day to discover that people, who insisted they were telling the truth all along, really were, and that nothing is as it seems any more. Role-play is reversed and we start to judge for ourselves.

Current alleged miscarriages of justice that ask you to judge for yourself on the basis of case evidence and a search for the truth:

Michael Stone, Eddie Guilfoyle, Samar Alami and Jawad Botmeh, Susan May, Sion Jenkins, Jamil Chowdary, Jake and Keith Mawhinney, Charles Hanson, Zoorah Shah, John Taft, Derek Christian, Barry George, Donna Anthony, Ian Thomas, Trevor Gardner, Anthony Nolan, Clare Barstow, Timothy Caines, Dorent Lord Francis, Terence Allen, Nicholas Tucker, Charles Rickards, Carol Hanson (RIP), James Hanratty (RIP), Darin Hobbs, Karl Watson, Richard Southern, Peter Hannigan, Ihsan Ulhaque, Sam Cole, Jimmy Ingram, Pippy Perry, Paul Lyons, Jong Rhee, Paul Cleeland, James Power, Graham Huckerby, Glynn Razell, Dai Morris, Kevin Lane, Miles Evans, Susan Shickle, Jonathan Probyn, Keith Beckles.

List of honour:

Guildford Four, Maguire Seven, Birmingham Six, M25 Three, Timothy Evans (RIP), Stefan Kiszko (RIP), Bridgewater Four, Eddie Browning, Darvell Brothers, Taylor Sisters, Cardiff Three, Gary Mills and Tony Poole, John McGranaghan, Stephen Downing, Frank Johnson, Paddy Nicholls, Johnny Kamara, Robert Brown, Reg Dudley and Bob Maynard, Mary Druhan, Ian Gordon, Sheila Bowler, Danny McNamee, Sara Thornton, Sally Clark, Peter Fell, Robert Haughton, David Ryan

James, Judith Ward, Derek Bentley (RIP), Derek Treadaway, Cardiff Newsagent Three, Mark Cleary, Hussein Mattan (RIP), John Hemphill, Alex Allan, Ashley King, Trevor Campbell, Trevor McCalla, Andrew Evans, George Long, Andrew Smith, Keith Twitchell, John Roberts, Patricia Bass, Richard Karling, Dudley Higgins, Collin Wallice, Alexander Hall, Patrick Irvine, Roger Beardmore, John Brannan (RIP) and Bernard Murphy, George Lewis, Kevin Callan (RIP), Jonathon Jones, Winston Silcott, David Asbury, Jan Christofides, Christopher Hagans, John Wilson, John Cummiskey, Roy Mends, Michael Magee, Charlie Smith, George Kelly, Trevor Wickens, David Cooper, Michael Shirley, Michael McMahon, Terence Pinfold, Harry MacKenney, Russell Stuart Causley, Shane Stepon Smith, Angela Cannings, Shokat Chenia, T. C. Campbell, Joe Steel.

INDEX